MEDITERRA DIET COOKBOOK

THE ULTIMATE MEDITERRANEAN DIET FOR BEGINNERS WITH 21 DAY MEAL PLAN

AMZ PUBLISHING

TABLE OF CONTENTS

LUNCH RECIPES 48

DINNER RECIPES 69

67

SNACKS RECIPES 89

Introduction

What is the Mediterranean Diet?

W̲hen one reads the word "Mediterranean," one tends to think of the sea. This brings to mind seafood. The diet has its roots in the Mediterranean basin, a land that has historically been called a powerhouse of societal evolution. This area in the Nile valley was good land for the people of the East and West.

The frequent interaction of people from different regions and cultures had a large effect on customs, languages, religion, and perspectives and had a transformative effect on lifestyles. This cultural integration and clash further affected eating habits.

Looking at the food content of the Mediterranean diet, one can see the reflection of diverse cultures and classes. Bread, wine, and oil reflect agriculture; this is further complemented by vegetables like lettuce, mushrooms, and mallow. There is little preference for meat but much preference for fish and seafood. This shows the gluttonous nature of people from Rome. Here we also get the Germanic flavor of pig's meat with garden vegetables. The beer was made with grains.

The food culture of bread, wine, and oil went beyond the Germanic and Christian Roman culture and entered the boundaries of the Arabs. The reason was their existence at the southern shore of the Mediterranean. Their food culture was unique because of the variety of leafy vegetables they grew. They had eggplants, spinach, sugarcane, and fruits like oranges, citrus, lemon, and pomegranate. This influenced the cooking style of the Latins and affected their recipes.

The big geographical event that is the discovery of America by Europeans has a great additional impact on the Mediterranean diet. This event added a range of new foodstuffs like beans, potatoes, tomatoes, chili, and peppers. Tomato, the red plant, was first ornamental and later considered edible. It further became an important part of the Mediterranean diet.

The historical analysis of the Mediterranean diet shows how the feeding of the Egyptians to the discovery of America gave us the Mediterranean diet of today. The nutritional model of the Mediterranean diet is intimately related to the Mediterranean people, lifestyle, and history.

There are some established health and cultural platforms, like UNESCO, which define the Mediterranean diet, unfolding the meaning of word "diet," which has come from the word "diata," meaning lifestyle or way of life.

It focuses on the journey of food from the landscape to the table, covering cuisine, harvesting, processing, preparation, fishing, cooking, and a specific way of consumption.

There is a variation in the Mediterranean diet in different countries due to ethnic and cultural differences, diverse religions, and economic disparity. As per the description and recommendation of dieticians and food experts, the Mediterranean diet has the following proportion of foods. In cereals, there are whole grains and legumes. For fats, olive oil is a major source. Onion, garlic, tomatoes, and leafy vegetables and peppers are major greens. Fresh fruits are major in snacks and desserts. Eggs, milk, yogurt, and other dairy products are taken moderately. Food items like red meat, processed food, and refined sugar are taken as little as possible.

This diet has a 25 % to 35% proportion of fat in terms of the calorie count and saturated fat is never beyond 8%. As far as oil is concerned, there are region-wise alternatives. In central and northern Italy, butter and lard are commonly used in cooking. Olive is used mainly for snacks and salad dressing.

This diet reflects the food pattern of Crete, the rest of Greece, and much of Italy in the early 1960s. It gained widespread recognition in the 1990s. There is an irony in the Mediterranean diet that although people living in this region tend to consume a high amount of fats, they enjoy far better cardiovascular health as compared to people of America who consume an equal amount of fat.

The tradition of the Mediterranean diet offers a cuisine rich in color, taste, flavor, and aroma. Most of all, it keeps us closer to nature. It may be simple in looks but rich in health and has much to offer that is in no way less than any other healthy diet. Some Americans describe the Mediterranean diet as all styles of homemade pasta with Parmesan sauce and enrichment with a few pieces of meat. It includes many fresh vegetables with just olive oil sprinkled on them. Desserts in this diet include fresh fruits.

A good Mediterranean diet does not include soybean, canola, or any other refined oil. There is no room for processed meat, refined sugar, white bread, refined grains, white pasta, or pizza dough containing white flour.

This diet is characterized by a balanced use of food items that have a high amount of fiber, unsaturated fats, and antioxidants. Also, there is an approach that gives health a priority by cutting the consumption of unhealthy animal fats and meat. This strikes a balance between the amount of energy intake and its consumption.

This magical diet is not just a preferred approach to health, with a wide range of magical recipes, but also a conduit between wide ranges of cultures. People of this region are sons of the soil and so is their food that comes from land and the soil. It can ensure, if consumed rationally, the efficacy of different bodily functions.

Some famous health organizations across the globe have designed food pyramids to make it clear as to what are the most common forms of the Mediterranean region. It became popular among health activists because people of this region have high life expectancy despite less access to health facilities. It has been stated by the American Heart Association and American Diabetes Association that the Mediterranean diet lowers the risk of cardiovascular disease and type 2 diabetes. If a patterned Mediterranean diet plan is followed, it may have a lasting effect on health and can help in reducing and maintaining a healthy weight.

An Appeal from the Publisher

Hello wonderful reader!

We hope you are enjoying this book.

We wanted to let you know that you have made an impact on many lives by reading this book.

Just to give you a brief introduction: We are a small publishing company with a team of 8 writers and 2 editors.

Most of our employees come from financially weaker section and our company is the only means they support their families. This is our way of giving back to the society.

We don't have the giant advertising budgets that many other publishers and businesses do online.

So, one way that you can really support our mission and our business is by leaving us a review on this book.

For a small company like us, getting reviews (especially on Amazon) means we can submit our books for advertising.

This means we can actually sell a few copies from time to time and make a bigger impact on the society as a whole. So, every review means a lot to us.

We can't THANK YOU enough for this!

What are the benefits of the Mediterranean Diet?

In this nutrition- and health-conscious world, medical scientists, nutritionists, and health scientists keep researching for healthy options and lifestyle changes that can ensure health and longevity along with agility. There is an emerging consensus among health experts that a diet that has fiber and a balanced amount of protein, healthy fats, and minerals can lead to optimum health and a healthy life. It can check cardiovascular diseases, diabetes, cancer, and stroke and help in maintaining a healthy weight.

The Mediterranean diet has all these attributes. Its ingredients are rich in plants, healthy fats, fruits, whole grains, healthy meat, and much more. As a matter of fact, it has all the elements which are essential to a healthy diet. There have been claims about its positive effect on health and physical well-being.

In a study conducted among 25,000 women across a period of 12 years, it has been established that those who consume the Mediterranean diet have a 25% lower chance of having cardiovascular disease. The reason behind this positive change is the decline in inflammation and blood glucose level, and an improved body mass index.

There is low saturated fat with a high amount of monounsaturated fats, protein, and dietary fiber. Olive oil has a major healthy element that is oleic acid. It is highly beneficial for the health of the human heart. It has the approval of the European Food Safety Authority Panel on Dietetic Products, Nutrition, and Allergies. It has been mentioned that its polyphenols protect the oxidation of lipids in the blood. This happens because of priority being given to olive oil, which has oleic acid that helps in maintaining normal LDL in the blood and may check cardiovascular diseases. It has also been claimed by the American Heart Association that consumption of olive oil can be an aid to maintaining cardiovascular health. If this diet is followed, the intake of refined breads, processed foods, and unhealthy meat gets reduced. The diet also recommends replacing hard liquor with red wine. This way, it can reduce the risk of cardiovascular diseases.

This diet has high fiber content. This reduces the glucose level in the blood and checks the causes which develop type 2 diabetes. This fiber makes one feel full and keeps cravings under control. This also helps in keeping weight under check and reduces constipation and helps regulate bowel movement.

Maintaining a healthy weight is a key factor to good health. It becomes easy to maintain an ideal weight when a fruit- and vegetable-rich diet is taken. The icing on the cake is the total absence of refined sugar and white flour. When combined with a physical routine, it becomes easy to maintain a healthy weight. This may help in reducing obesity as well. Moreover, maintaining an ideal weight can give us multiple health benefits.

It has been found through comprehensive research that regular and monitored consumption of the Mediterranean diet can reduce the risk of death from cancer by five to six percent. This has been confirmed in a study conducted on cancer patients in 2017. It has also been found that the Mediterranean diet may decrease the chances of cancer.

Stress is the key factor affecting life adversely today. The Mediterranean diet can be a relaxant here. It has been found in various studies that a sincere adherence to the Mediterranean diet can check the impairment of cognitive ability. It does so by improving good cholesterol, levels of blood sugar, and the overall health of blood vessels. This, as a result, reduces your risk of dementia or Alzheimer's disease.

The Mediterranean diet, with maximum vegetables, fruits, and nuts in it, is rich in antioxidants, vitamins, and other nutrients. This protects cells from damage that otherwise occurs if there is oxidative stress. Consequently, it reduces the risk of Parkinson's disease by fifty percent. Adhering to this diet can also lower the causes of depression and give a healthier state of mind.

It has been noticed, in a study conducted by food scientists on women who had chances of stroke in the United Kingdom, that when they followed the Mediterranean diet very strictly, it reduced their chances of getting stroke by twenty percent. However, it was not so in men. Clinical research is underway to observe its effect on the male gender as well.

The National Institute on Aging funded a small study on aging which was published in 2018. The journal highlighted how the brain scans of 70 persons showed that people who strictly adhered to the Mediterranean diet did not show any sign of aging, while those who had a preference for other forms of diet had a plaque pattern which adds to the adverse effect of aging. This shows that the Mediterranean diet adds longevity to human life and gives lasting health. The lungs play an important role in oxygenating our body but with age, their inhalation ability impairs. Whole grains, dairy products, and fish can improve the ability of the lungs to perform better. Further, those who remain disciplined and steadfast in taking the Mediterranean diet have a 22-29% lower chance of getting hearing loss.

It is an obvious fact that the Mediterranean diet has an ample amount of nutrients and that if we consume this diet, it helps in the prevention of muscle damage, boosts muscle strength, and enhances agility. This improves the efficiency of the brain. This means consumers of this diet have better thinking and learning abilities, improved memory, and much better concentration.

This diet is quite beneficial for kidney patients and those who have undergone a kidney transplant. In studies, it has been found that the diet can reduce the risk of kidney dysfunction. Further, it can bring down graft failure by as much as 32% and its loss by 26% in patients who undergo kidney transplants.

If a person develops inflammatory bowel diseases like piles, the Mediterranean diet can cause a cure. It has been found, after studies and case histories, that consumers of this diet are 57% less prone to develop Crohn's disease.

The benefits are multiple and nutritionists are still counting them.

How to get started?

The best way to cause a change is to start it. But the biggest question is how to start. The situation is much better if what we are to start has multiple benefits. The Mediterranean diet obviously falls in this category, where the advantages outnumber the limitations it may force on our lifestyle.

If you feel that it is difficult to change your diet, you can choose alternatives that work well and can help you switch to a healthier option. Here are certain ways that can help you switch to the Mediterranean diet.

It is good to start by keeping vegetables and fruits at the upper ladder in your list of priorities and giving sausages and pepperoni in salad dressing a backseat. You can start by giving a plate of tomato slices a try. It should be given just a drizzle of olive oil and mashed feta cheese. Soups, crudité plates, and salads can be awesome starters.

Skipping breakfast may seem effective but it can put an extra burden on your system to keep you going. On the other hand, whole grains, fruits, and other foods that are rich in fiber can be an effective way to start your day. Moreover, it will keep you filled and your cravings at bay.

Replace usual calorie-loaded desserts like cake, ice cream, pastries, etc. with fruits like apples, grapes, fresh figs, or strawberries. This will make you digest better and stay lighter. A refreshing feeling will work as motivation and keep you adherent to this magical diet.

If you leap to change, it may never happen. There is a famous saying: "A thousand-mile journey starts with a single step." This is quite applicable to shifting to the Mediterranean diet. You can start with small steps like sautéeing with olive oil and eating more vegetables and fruits in your salad. Replace your snacks with fruits. Similarly, other heavy dishes can be substituted for veggies.

Choose skimmed milk or milk with 2% fats over full-fat milk. This will make you feel lighter and healthier. As a result, it will work as a motivating factor for opting for the Mediterranean diet. The change in energy level and nutrition will work as a triggering factor and driving force.

It is said that if it is easy, it is achievable. The most accessible is to use whole grains in place of refined grains. Your choice should be whole-wheat bread and not white bread that is made of refined flour. Similarly, brown rice or wild rice should replace white rice. Sometimes it is difficult to choose authentic whole grains. It is easy now, however, as a black and gold stamp has been developed by the Oldways Whole Grain Council to select quality over paste.

Ancient grains or whole grains form an important part of the Mediterranean diet. There is a huge variety of these grains. These are amaranth, faro, millet, spelt, and the believably Egyptian kamut; yet another is teff, which is similar to poppy seeds in its size. You can try one seed at a time. Slowly and steadily, you can move to more options. Each seed has its own flavor and texture. The good news is that these whole grains have become quite popular and are quite common. Consequently, these are now available in mainstream restaurants as well. This means you can try it and then make it a part of your diet.

If you make up your mind to go for it, you should take at least six servings a day. Half of it should be of whole grains. It may be worrisome to some because of carbs but you can throw your caution to the wind because it, for sure, will cause long-term benefits. You should not overlook the fact that quick loss of weight may not be healthy.

So, whole grain in the Mediterranean diet is the best option.
You may not be able to swap your current diet with the Mediterranean diet at once. So, try one meal based on vegetables, whole grains, and beans. Use spices and herbs to add a palatable punch.

If you are protein-conscious and remain worried about it in your diet, your dependence on meat might end by giving room to lentils in your diet. Lentils are sources of high protein and have much fiber, too. Beans have an edge, as these have ample antioxidants. How motivating!

Stock your pantry with handy ingredients. These ingredients should be easy to use. Some of them can be popular protein sources like lentils, chickpeas, and beans. Lentils require only 25 minutes of cooking time without any need for overnight soaking. As for chickpeas and canned beans, you only need to rinse them; then you can put them into soups, burgers, salads, sandwiches, and much more.

Giving up meat altogether may be a challenge but you can give it a start by taking meat in small proportions. Use small pieces of chicken or lean meat slices. You can stir fry your dish and avoid deep frying.

This will keep it less oil-soaked and more nourishing. It is good news for fish eaters, as when they are on the Mediterranean diet, they can eat two servings of salmon, sardines, and tuna, which are essential to the Mediterranean diet. There may be a risk of mercury but in the opinion of American nutritionists, the benefits outweigh the risk. The variety of fish mentioned here has a comparatively lower amount of mercury.

Dairy products are also a great protein source. Greek yogurt is a great option but it should be eaten in moderation.

In short, the Mediterranean diet is a healthy option with a wide range of tasty choices. If you start with an easy approach, taking small steps at a time, making little changes in your meal plans, you can go a long way.

21 DAY
MEAL
PLAN

Day 1	Day 2	Day 3
Breakfast: Spinach and Artichoke Frittata **Lunch:** Mediterranean Chickpea Quinoa Bowl **Snacks:** 15-Minute Mediterranean Chickpea Salad **Dinner:** Mediterranean Portobello Mushroom Pizzas with Arugula Salad	**Breakfast:** Hearty Breakfast Fruit Salad **Lunch:** Harissa Chickpea Stew With Eggplant and Millet **Snacks:** Lemon Herb Mediterranean Pasta Salad **Dinner:** Slow-Cooker Mediterranean Quinoa with Arugula	**Breakfast:** Shakshuka **Lunch:** Five-Minute Heirloom Tomato Toast **Snacks:** Hummus **Dinner:** Walnut-Rosemary Crusted Salmon
Day 4	Day 5	Day 6
Breakfast: Balsamic Berries with Honey Yogurt **Lunch:** Eggplant and Herb Flatbread **Snacks:** Mini Greek Pita Pizzas **Dinner:** Mediterranean Stuffed Chicken Breasts	**Breakfast:** Caprese Avocado Toast **Lunch:** 15-Minute Mediterranean Couscous with Tuna and Pepperoncini **Snacks:** Healthy Avocado Cilantro White Bean Dip **Dinner:** Charred Shrimp and Pesto Buddha Bowls	**Breakfast:** Spinach Feta Breakfast Wraps **Lunch:** Pesto Quinoa Bowls With Roasted Veggies and Labneh **Snacks:** Homemade Granola Bars Recipe (Gluten-Free, Vegan, Dairy-Free) **Dinner:** Sheet-Pan Salmon with Sweet Potatoes and Broccoli
Day 7	Day 8	Day 9
Breakfast: Easy Homemade Muesli **Lunch:** Greek Yogurt Chicken Salad Stuffed Peppers **Snacks:** Peach Caprese Skewers **Dinner:** Greek Cauliflower Rice Bowls with Grilled Chicken	**Breakfast:** Kale and Goat Cheese Frittata Cups **Lunch:** 15-Minute Mezze Plate with Toasted Za'atar Pita Bread **Snacks:** Charcuterie Bistro Lunch Box **Dinner:** Prosciutto Pizza with Corn and Arugula	**Breakfast:** Easy, Fluffy Lemon Ricotta Pancakes **Lunch:** Greek Lemon Chicken Skewers With Tzatziki Sauce **Snacks:** Hummus, Feta and Bell Pepper Cracker **Dinner:** Vegan Mediterranean Lentil Soup

Day 10	Day 11	Day 12
Breakfast: Smashed Egg Toasts with Herby Lemon Yogurt **Lunch:** Eggplant Pizza **Snacks:** Tomato-Basil Skewers **Dinner:** BBQ Shrimp with Garlicky Kale and Parmesan-Herb Couscous	**Breakfast:** Mediterranean Breakfast Pitas **Lunch:** Cold Lemon Zoodles **Snacks:** Marinated Olives and Feta **Dinner:** Green Shakshuka with Spinach, Chard, and Feta	**Breakfast:** Crispy White Beans with Greens and Poached Egg **Lunch:** Stuffed Eggplant **Snacks:** Garlic Hummus **Dinner:** One-Skillet Salmon with Fennel and Sun-Dried Tomato Couscous
Day 13	Day 14	Day 15
Breakfast: Breakfast Grain Salad with Blueberries, Hazelnuts, and Lemon **Lunch:** Wild Alaska Salmon and Smashed Cucumber Grain Bowls **Snacks:** Clementine and Pistachio Ricotta **Dinner:** Chicken and Spinach Skillet Pasta with Lemon and Parmesan	**Breakfast:** Eggs with Summer Tomatoes, Zucchini, and Bell Peppers **Lunch:** Harissa Potato Salad **Snacks:** Ricotta and Yogurt Parfait **Dinner:** Baked chicken and Ricotta Meatballs	**Breakfast:** Avocado and Egg Breakfast Pizza **Lunch:** Greek Lemon Chicken Soup **Snacks:** Mediterranean Picnic Snacks **Dinner:** Chickpea Vegetable Coconut Curry

Day 16	Day 17	Day 18
Breakfast: Mediterranean Breakfast Sandwich **Lunch:** Mediterranean Bento Lunch **Snacks:** Crockpot Chunky Monkey Paleo Trail Mix **Recipe** **Dinner:** Broccoli Rabe and Burrata with Lemon	**Breakfast:** Breakfast Hash with Brussels sprouts and Sweet Potatoes **Lunch:** Greek Meatball Mezze Bowls **Snacks:** Savory Feta Spinach and Sweet Red Pepper **Muffins** **Dinner:** Tomato Poached Cod with Special Herbs	**Breakfast:** Mediterranean Keto Low-Carb Egg Muffins with Ham **Lunch:** Mediterranean Chicken with Orzo Salad **Snacks:** Smoked Salmon, Avocado, and Cucumber Bites **Dinner:** Chickpea Shawarma Salad
Day 19	Day 20	Day 21
Breakfast: Spinach and Artichoke Frittata **Lunch:** Mediterranean Chickpea Quinoa Bowl **Snacks:** 15 Minute Mediterranean Chickpea Salad **Dinner:** Mediterranean Portobello Mushroom Pizzas with Arugula Salad	**Breakfast:** Hearty Breakfast Fruit Salad **Lunch:** Harissa Chickpea Stew With Eggplant and Millet **Snacks:** Lemon Herb Mediterranean Pasta Salad **Dinner:** Slow-Cooker Mediterranean Quinoa with Arugula	**Breakfast:** Shakshuka **Lunch:** Five-Minute Heirloom Tomato Toast **Snacks:** Hummus **Dinner:** Walnut-Rosemary Crusted Salmon

BREAKFAST RECIPES

AVOCADO AND EGG BREAKFAST PIZZA

Serving size: 1
Servings per recipe: 4
Calories: 337
Preparation time: 10 minutes
Cooking time: 15 minutes

Carbs: 33.2 g Proteins: 12.3 g Fats: 17.6 g

INGREDIENTS

- Large Hass avocado - 1
- Finely chopped cilantro - 1 tbsp
- Lime juice - 1½ tsp
- Salt - 1/8 tsp
- Pizza dough, homemade - ½ lb
- Large eggs - 4
- Vegetable oil - 1 tbsp
- Hot sauce, for serving (optional)

DIRECTIONS

1. Cut avocado in half lengthwise after removing pit with a spoon. Scoop the flesh and put it into a bowl. Now add lemon juice, cilantro, and salt. Mash a few pieces of avocado using a fork until smooth. Taste and adjust the flavor. If the avocado is bigger, more salt and lime juice may be required.

2. Divide dough into 4 pieces of equal size. Now roll each piece into a slim 6-inch circle. Try again if the dough does not stay at a point.

3. Over a medium flame, heat a well-seasoned cast-iron skillet. Now place one dough circle in the center of the skillet. Cook for 1-2 minutes or until the underside is brown and the upper side is bubbly. Repeat the procedure by flipping the dough circle. Press with a spatula if puffing is seen in the dough top. It may seem burnt in spots but it's ok. Transfer to a platter and repeat with the remaining dough circles.

4. On each cooked piece of dough, spread the avocado mixture.

5. Over the medium flame, heat oil in the skillet. Now fry eggs to the desired level and place them on top of the pizza. Serve at once, with or without hot sauce.

BALSAMIC BERRIES WITH HONEY YOGURT

Serving size: 4
Calories: 111
Preparation time: 15
Cooking time: 10 minutes

Carbs: 18 g Proteins: 4.6 g Fats: 3 g

INGREDIENTS

- Strawberries, hulled and halved, or quartered if very large - 8 oz. (about 1½ cups)
- Blueberries - 1 cup
- Raspberries - 1 cup
- Balsamic vinegar - 1 tbsp
- Whole-milk plain Greek yogurt - ⅔ cup
- Honey - 2 tsp

DIRECTIONS

1. In a large bowl, toss raspberries, blueberries, and strawberries with balsamic vinegar. Leave for about 10 minutes.
2. Now, in a small bowl, stir yogurt and honey.
3. Next, part berries as per the number of serving bowls. Top with a drop of honey yogurt mix.

BREAKFAST GRAIN SALAD WITH BLUEBERRIES, HAZELNUTS, AND LEMON

Serving size: 2
Servings per recipe: 8
Calories: 353
Preparation time: 5 minutes
Cooking time: 25 minutes

Carbs: 38 g Proteins: 9.3 g Fats: 20.1 g

INGREDIENTS

- Steel-cut oats - 1 cup
- Dry golden quinoa - 1 cup
- Dry millet - ½ cup
- Olive oil, divided - 3 tbsp
- Piece fresh ginger, peeled and cut into coins - 1 (1-inch)
- Large lemons, zest, and juice - 2
- Maple syrup - ½ cup
- Greek yogurt (or soy yogurt, if you want to make this vegan) - 1 cup
- Nutmeg - ¼ tsp
- Hazelnuts, roughly chopped and toasted - 2 cups
- Blueberries or mixed berries - 2 cups

DIRECTIONS

1. In a fine-mesh strainer, mix millet, oats, and quinoa. For a minute, rinse under running water. Set aside.

2. Over medium flame in a 3-quart saucepan, heat 1 tbsp olive oil. Add rinsed millet, oats, and quinoa. Cook for 2-3 minutes. Add 4 ½ cups of water and stir in ¾ tsp. salt, zest of a lemon, and ginger coins.

3. Bring the water to a boil. After covering, turn down the heat and simmer for about 20 minutes. Turn the burner off and leave for 5 minutes. Remove the lid and touch lightly with a fork. Take off the ginger. On a large baking sheet, spread grains. Allow it cool for a minimum of half an hour.

4. With a spoon, put the cooled grain into a large bowl. Stir in the zest of the second lemon.

5. Whisk the remaining olive oil (2 tbsp) in a mid-sized bowl with the juice of 2 lemons. Wait until emulsified. Mix yogurt, maple syrup, and nutmeg. Pour this into grains and stir until coated well. Add in blueberries and hazelnuts. Taste and flavor with salt, if required. For better flavor, refrigerate overnight.

BREAKFAST HASH WITH BRUSSELS SPROUTS AND SWEET POTATOES

Serving Size:1
Servings per recipe: 4
Calories: 206
Preparation time: 10 minutes
Cooking time: 25 minutes

Carbs: 19.3 g Proteins: 9.7 g Fats: 11 g

INGREDIENTS

SWEET POTATO & BRUSSELS SPROUTS

- Medium-large sweet potato, chopped into bite-size pieces (skin on) - 1
- Brussels sprouts (quartered if large, halved if small) - 3 cups
- Avocado oil (or other neutral oil // or sub water if avoiding oil) - 1 tbsp
- Each sea salt and black pepper - 1 healthy pinch

INGREDIENTS

THE REST

- Avocado oil (or other neutral oil // or sub water if avoiding oil) - 2 tsp
- Medium yellow, white, or red onion, finely chopped - ½
- Minced garlic cloves - 3
- Finely diced Fuji or Jonagold apple (peeling optional // seeds + stem removed) - ¾ cup
- Fresh minced sage (or sub dried) - 1 tbsp
- Dried currants (optional) - 2 tbsp
- Spicy chicken or pork sausage (optional // buy local and organic meat- 1 cup whenever possible // or sub-Vegan Sausage)
- Fresh spinach - 2 heaping cups
- Large eggs (farm fresh or organic, free-range / pasture-raised whenever possible // see notes for vegan options*)- 4

DIRECTIONS

1. With parchment paper, line a baking sheet and preheat the oven to 400°F.
2. Put Brussels sprouts and sweet potato on a baking sheet. Drizzle oil, flavor with pepper and salt, and toss for coating. Bake for 22-28 minutes. Toss at mid-point for even cooking.
3. By that time, over medium flame, heat a large skillet. Once it is hot, add oil and onion. Sauté for around a minute. Then add apple, garlic, sage, and currants. Sauté for around 3 minutes or to the point of turning golden brown and aromatic. Stir in-between.
4. Add sausage and keep sautéing until golden brown and thoroughly cooked—5-8 minutes. Stir constantly and use a spoon to break sausage into small pieces.
5. Once the sausage is cooked, add spinach, cover skillet, and cook for a few minutes until tender. Add in and stir roasted Brussels sprouts and sweet potato. Turn off heat and set aside until serving.
6. Over a medium flame, heat a separate skillet. After it is hot, add the number of eggs as desired.
7. In the pan, crack an egg and cook for 3 minutes uncovered. Cover with a lid and leave for 1-2 minutes to help the white cook and keep the yolk soft.
8. Garnish with hot sauce and fresh herbs. Store cooled-down leftovers covered in the fridge for 3-4 days. In the freezer, they can be kept for a month.

CAPRESE AVOCADO TOAST

Serving size: 2
Servings per recipe: 2
Calories: 649
Preparation time: 4 minutes
Cooking time: 7-8 minutes

Carbs: 86.4 g Proteins: 23.9 g Fats: 24.6 g

INGREDIENTS

- Slices hearty sandwich bread, such as peasant bread, sourdough, whole-wheat, or multi-grain - 2
- Medium avocado, halved and pit removed - 1
- Grape tomatoes, halved - 8
- Fresh ciliegine or bite-sized mozzarella balls - 2 oz. (about 12)
- Large fresh basil leaves, torn - 4
- Balsamic glaze - 2 tbsp

DIRECTIONS

1. First, toast the bread. Meanwhile, mash the avocado in a small bowl.
2. Over the toast, spread mashed avocado. Use tomatoes, mozzarella balls, and basil leaves to top each slice. Then sprinkle balsamic glaze. Serve at once.

CRISPY WHITE BEANS WITH GREENS AND POACHED EGG

Serving size: 4
Servings per recipe: 2
Calories: 301
Preparation time: 5 minutes
Cooking time: 15 minutes

Carbs: 26.5 g Proteins: 15.5 g Fats: 15.5 g

INGREDIENTS

- Olive oil, divided - 3 tbsp
- Can cannellini beans, drained and rinsed - 1 (15-ounce)
- Kosher salt, divided - 1 tsp
- Za'atar, divided - 2 tsp
- Medium bunch Swiss chard (about 10 oz.), stems removed and leaves thinly sliced 1
- Garlic, minced - 2 cloves
- Red pepper flakes, plus more for serving - ¼ tsp
- Freshly squeezed lemon juice - 1 tbsp
- Large eggs, poached - 4

DIRECTIONS

1. In a large frying pan, heat 2 tbsp oil over medium heat. Keep until shimmering. Spread the beans into an even layer. Cook until light brown at the bottom. It generally takes 2-4 minutes. Add 1 tsp za'tar and ½ tsp salt. Stir to combine. Spread the beans again and cook, stirring until beans turn golden brown and bubble on all sides.

2. Put the rest of 1 tbsp oil on the pan. Add chard, rest of ½ tsp salt and 1 tsp za'atar, red pepper flakes, and garlic. Stir in between and keep cooking until the chard gets soft. Take the pan off the flame, add lemon juice, and toss well.

3. In 4 bowls, divide beans and greens. Top each with a poached egg and a bit more of the red pepper flakes.

EASY, FLUFFY LEMON RICOTTA PANCAKES

Serving size: 4
Servings per recipe: 12
Calories: 344
Preparation time: 10 minutes
Cooking time: 15-18 minutes

Carbs: 32.3 g Proteins: 17.7 g Fats: 15.9 g

INGREDIENTS

- Large eggs - 4
- Medium lemon - 1
- Whole-milk ricotta cheese - 1 cup
- Whole or 2% milk - ½ cup
- All-purpose flour - 1 cup
- Granulated sugar - 1 tbsp
- Baking powder - 1 tsp
- Kosher salt - ¼ tsp
- Unsalted butter, for cooking

DIRECTIONS

1. Mix white and yolk of the 4 large eggs with an electric hand mixer in a medium-sized bowl.
2. Grate zest of a medium-sized lemon over the yolks. Squeeze lemon juice into the bowl. Now add ½ whole or 2% milk and 1 cup whole-milk ricotta cheese. Whisk to combine. Next, add 1 cup all-purpose flour, 1 tsp baking powder, sugar (granulated), and ¼ tsp kosher salt, and mix well to combine.
3. At mid-high speed, beat egg whites until stiff peaks form. Stir ⅓ of beaten egg whites into yolk batter using a rubber spatula. Gently fold the remaining egg whites to combine well.
4. On medium flame, heat a non-stick skillet. Coat with 1 tsp unsalted butter. Put batter into pan ¼ cup at a time (you can use a spatula to spread a round of 4 inches each). Keep cooking until surface bubbles appear, the edges look dry, and the bottom turns golden brown. Flip and cook until golden brown.
5. The pancakes can now be transferred to a warm plate or oven.

EASY HOMEMADE MUESLI

Serving size: 1
Servings per recipe: 8
Calories: 275
Preparation time: 15 minutes
Cooking time: 15 minutes

Carbs: 36 g Proteins: 8.5 g Fats: 13.4 g

INGREDIENTS

- Rolled oats - 3 ½ cups
- Wheat bran - ½ cup
- Kosher salt - ½ tsp
- Ground cinnamon - ½ tsp
- Sliced almonds ½ cup
- Raw pecans, coarsely chopped - ¼ cup
- Raw pepitas (shelled pumpkin seeds) - ¼ cup
- Unsweetened coconut flakes - ½ cup
- Dried apricots, coarsely chopped - ¼ cup
- Dried cherries - ¼ cup

DIRECTIONS

1. To divide the oven into thirds, arrange 2 racks and heat to 350°F. Put wheat bran, salt, cinnamon, and oats on a rimmed baking sheet. Spread an even layer. On the second rimmed baking sheet, put pecans, pepitas, and almonds. Toss to combine and spread evenly in a layer. Both baking sheets should be transferred to the oven, with oats on the top part of the rack and nuts on the bottom.
2. Set aside the baking sheet with nuts to cool. Spatter coconut powder over oats. Bake the upper rack until coconut is golden brown, preferably 5 minutes. Remove from oven and cool for 10 minutes.
3. Move the contents of both baking sheets into a large bowl.
4. Put cherries and apricots to combine well; toss.
5. You can store muesli in an airtight container at room temperature for a month.
6. You can have it with cereals, yogurt, and oatmeal or with drops of honey.

EGGS WITH SUMMER TOMATOES, ZUCCHINI, AND BELL PEPPERS

Serving size: 1
Servings per recipe: 2
Calories: 226
Preparation time: 5 minutes
Cooking time: 30-35 minutes

Carbs: 20.6 g Proteins: 11.1 g Fats: 12.5 g

INGREDIENTS

- Olive oil - 1 tbsp
- Small yellow onion, halved and thinly sliced - 1
- Garlic, minced - 1 clove
- Medium summer squash or zucchini - (approximately 4 cups) 2
- Medium tomatoes, chopped - (approximately 3 cups) 2
- Fresh thyme (optional) - ½ tsp
- Ground Spanish piquillo pepper or Spanish paprika - 1 tsp
- Medium red bell pepper - 1
- Salt and pepper - 1 tbsp each
- Large eggs - 2

DIRECTIONS

1. In a large heavy skillet, heat olive oil at medium heat. Add sliced onions. Keep stirring to the point of translucence. Next, add garlic and cook for a minute. Add squash and cook for 10 minutes or until soft. Then add thyme (optional) and piquillo. Allow simmering to the point of even cooking, when it turns stewy, for around 20 minutes.

2. Keep cooking ratatouille. Meanwhile, on the stovetop, roast the pepper. Once cool, take off the core and seed. Cut into 1-inch pieces. Now put the skillet off the flame, add roasted peppers, and add pepper and salt as per your taste. It is best to serve the dish warm.

3. Fry or boil eggs as per your choice. Divide veggies onto two plates and add a topping of eggs. You can serve it with buttered toast.

HEARTY BREAKFAST FRUIT SALAD

Serving size: 1
Servings per recipe: 5
Calories: 282
Preparation time: 10 minutes
Cooking time: 1 hour 20 minutes

Carbs: 34.8 g Proteins: 3.7 g Fats: 16.6 g

INGREDIENTS

- Pearl or hulled barley or any sturdy whole grain - 1 cup
- Water - 3 cups
- Olive oil, divided - 3 tbsp
- Kosher salt - ½ tsp
- ½ large pineapple, peeled and cut into 1½- to 2-inch chunks - 2 to 1½ cups
- Medium tangerines or mandarin-6, or large oranges - 5 (about 1½ lbs total)

INGREDIENTS

- Pomegranate seeds - 1¼ cups
- Small bunch fresh mint - 1
-

FOR THE DRESSING:
- Honey or another sweetener - ⅓ cup
- Juice and finely grated zest of 1 lemon - about ¼ cup juice
- Juice and finely grated zest of 2 limes - about ¼ cup juice
- Kosher salt - ½ tsp
- Olive oil - ¼ cup
- Toasted hazelnut or nut oil - ¼ cup

FOR THE FRUIT:
- Half pineapple (large), peeled and cut into 1 1/2- to 2-inch chunks
- Medium mandarins or tangerines - 6, or oranges large - 5 (about 1 1/2 pounds total)
- Pomegranate seeds - 1 1/4 cups
- Fresh mint - 1 small bunch

DIRECTIONS

1. With parchment paper, line-rimmed baking sheets. In a strainer, wash barley under cold water until the water below is clear, for around 1 minute. Shake the strainer gently to drain off the excess water. On one of the prepared baking sheets, place barley and, using a spatula, spread out the grains into a single layer. Leave it be to completely dry for 3-4 minutes.

2. In a microwave or stovetop, warm the water, then set it aside.

3. In a medium saucepan, heat 2 tbsp oil on high heat until simmering. Add barley carefully and toast, stirring constantly, until it darkens a bit. It generally takes 1 minute to 90 seconds.

4. Add salt and warm water and bring it to a boil. Turn the heat to the lowest. Cover the pan and keep cooking until soft and most of the water has been absorbed, for around 40-50 minutes. Take the pot off the heat and leave it covered for 10 minutes. This way, the barley will steam and finish absorbing the water. Then prepare the mint, fruit, and dressing.

5. In one of the large containers, place the pineapple chunks. Peel and cut mandarins, tangerines, or oranges into segments. Remove as much of the bitter white pith as possible. Place these fruits in another container, cover, and refrigerate. Keep pomegranate seeds in a covered box separately and refrigerate.

DIRECTIONS

6.   Mince or slice the mint leaves thinly. Keep them in a covered container and refrigerate.

7.   In a medium bowl, whisk juice, honey, zest, and salt together. Drizzle in olive oil and nut oil, while whisking constantly until incorporated. You can cover and refrigerate or refrigerate in a jar.

8.   Move the cooked barley onto the second prepared baking sheet and spread it in a layer evenly. Leave to cool completely for around 10-20 minutes. Drizzle barley with leftover 1 tbsp of oil and mix to coat.

9.   Move barley to a large container. Cover the container and keep it in a refrigerator.

10. At the time of serving, scoop ⅔ cup of barley into each bowl. In each bowl add 6 pieces of pineapple, 10-12 orange segments, and ¼ cup pomegranate seeds. Now add 1-2 tbsp of the mint and 2-3 tbsp of dressing to each bowl. Stir to mix and coat it with the dressing.

KALE AND GOAT CHEESE FRITTATA CUPS

Serving size: 1 cup
Servings per recipe: 8 cups
Calories: 179
Preparation time: 5 minutes
Cooking time: 35-40 minutes

Carbs: 1.2 g Proteins: 10.0 g Fats: 14.7 g

INGREDIENTS

- Chopped lacinato kale - 2 cups
- Garlic clove, thinly sliced - 1
- Olive oil - 3 tbsp
- Red pepper flakes - ¼ tsp
- Large eggs - 8
- Salt - ¼ tsp
- Ground black pepper dash
- Dried thyme - ½ tsp
- Goat cheese, crumbled - ¼ cup

DIRECTIONS

1. Preheat the oven to 350°F. Remove the leaves from kale ribs to get the cups of kale. Now wash and leave the leaves to dry. Cut these leaves into ½-inch-wide strips.
2. Cook garlic in a non-stick skillet, preferably of 10 inches, in 1 tbsp of oil. Keep the flame at medium to high for 30 seconds. Now add kale and red pepper flakes, and keep cooking until soft. Generally, it takes around 2 minutes.
3. Beat eggs along with salt and pepper in a medium-sized bowl. Now add thyme and kale to the blended mixture.
4. Grease a 12-cup muffin tin with 2 tbsp olive oil. Spatter the tops with goat cheese. Bake for 25-30 minutes or until set in the center.
5. It tastes best if eaten warm. You can refrigerate the leftovers but consume them within a week.

MEDITERRANEAN BREAKFAST PITAS

Serving size: 1 filled pita
Servings per recipe: 4
Calories: 206
Preparation time: 5 minutes
Cooking time: 15 -20 minutes

Carbs: 22.9 g Proteins: 12 g Fats: 8.3 g

INGREDIENTS

- Large eggs, at room temperature - 4
- Salt to taste
- Whole-wheat pita bread with pockets, cut in half - ½ cup
- Hummus - 4 oz.
- Medium cucumber, thinly sliced into rounds - 2
- Large diced medium tomatoes,
- Fresh parsley leaves, coarsely chopped handful
- Freshly ground black pepper
- Hot sauce (optional)

DIRECTIONS

1. Fill a medium-sized pan with water. Bring water to a boil. Place room-temperature eggs in this water and cook for around 7 minutes. Next, drain the hot water and place the eggs under a running tap of cold water. Now peel these eggs and make slices of ¼ inch thickness. Sprinkle salt.

2. Spread 2 tbsp of hummus inside each pita. Put diced tomatoes and cucumber slices into every pita. Sprinkle with salt and pepper. In each pita, tuck a sliced egg and sprinkle with hot sauce and parsley.

MEDITERRANEAN BREAKFAST SANDWICH

Serving size: 1
Servings per recipe: 4
Calories: 242
Preparation time: 15 minutes
Cooking time: 5 minutes

Carbs: 25 g Proteins: 13 g Fats: 11.7 g

INGREDIENTS

- Multigrain sandwich thins - 4
- Olive oil - 4 tsp
- Snipped fresh rosemary 1 tbsp or dried rosemary - ½ tsp
- Eggs - 4
- Fresh baby spinach leaves - 2 cups
- Medium tomato cut into - 8 slices 1
- Reduced-fat feta cheese - 4 tbsp
- Kosher salt - 1/8 tsp
- Freshly ground black pepper

DIRECTIONS

1. Heat the oven beforehand to 375°F. Now cut the sandwich thins. Next, brush the cut sides using 2 tsp of olive oil. Keep the toast on a baking sheet and put it in the oven for about 5 minutes or until the edges are light brown and crispy.

2. Over medium-high, heat 2 tsp olive oil and, over medium, heat the rosemary. Break eggs, one at a time, into the skillet. Cook until whites are set but yolks are quite runny or for 1 minute. With a spatula, break yolks. Flip the eggs and cook on another side until done. Remove from the heat.

3. Now place the bottom half of the toasted sandwich on the 4 serving plates. Divide spinach among sandwich thins on plates. Top each with tomato slices, an egg, and 1 tbsp of feta cheese. Sprinkle with pepper and salt. Now top each with the other sandwich thin halves.

MEDITERRANEAN KETO LOW-CARB EGG MUFFINS WITH HAM

Serving size: 2
Servings per recipe: 6
Calories: 109 kcal
Preparation time: 10
Cooking time: 15

Carbs: 1.8 g Proteins: 9.3 g Fats: 6.7 g

INGREDIENTS

- Slices of thin-cut deli ham - 9
- Canned roasted red pepper, sliced + additional for garnish - ½ cup
- Fresh spinach, minced - ⅓ cup
- Feta cheese, crumbled - ¼ cup
- Large eggs - 5
- Pinch of salt
- Pinch of pepper
- Pesto sauce - 1½ tbsp
- Fresh basil for garnish

DIRECTIONS

1. Preheat oven to 400°F. Profusely spray a muffin tin with cooking spray.
2. For each piece of the muffin tin to be lined with 1.5 pieces of ham, ensure that no place is left for the egg mixture to fall out.
3. In the bottom of each muffin tin, put a little bit of red pepper.
4. On the top of each red pepper, put 1 tbsp of minced spinach.
5. Top off pepper and spinach with a heaping ½ tbsp of crumbled feta cheese.
6. Whisk the eggs, salt, and pepper. Now divide the mixture of eggs equally among 6 muffin tins.
7. Bake until the eggs are puffy and are set for around 15-17 minutes.
8. After removing each cup from the muffin tin, garnish it with ¼ tsp of pesto sauce. Additionally, you can add roasted red pepper slices and fresh basil.

SHAKSHUKA

Serving size: 4
Servings per recipe: 6
Calories: 146
Preparation time: 10
Cooking time: 25 to 30 minutes

Carbs: 7.8 g Proteins: 7.9 g Fats: 9.7 g

INGREDIENTS

- Whole peeled tomatoes - 1 (28-ounce) can
- Olive oil - 2 tbsp
- Finely chopped small yellow onion - 1
- Tomato paste - 2 tbsp
- Harissa - 1 tbsp
- Garlic, minced - 3 cloves
- Ground cumin - 1 tsp
- Kosher salt - ½ tsp
- Large eggs - 6
- Loosely packed chopped fresh cilantro leaves and tender stems - ¼ cup
- Feta cheese, crumbled (optional)- 2 oz.

DIRECTIONS

1. In a large bowl, pour tomatoes as well as their juice. Crush with hands carefully. The pieces should be bite-sized.
2. In a skillet, heat oil for 10-12 minutes on medium flame. Now add onion and sauté for 5 minutes or until soft. Add harissa, garlic, cumin, tomato paste, and salt. Sauté until aromatic.
3. After adding tomatoes, simmer until the sauce slightly thickens (10 minutes).
4. Now remove the skillet from the stove. Make 6 small holes in the sauce and crack an egg into each.
5. Spoon a little sauce over each egg. If you expose the yolks, the white of the egg will cook faster.
6. For even cooking of eggs, keep rotating the pan until the white sets. It generally takes 8-12 minutes.
7. Remove the pan from the flame. Sprinkle feta and cilantro. Your dish is ready to be served with bread or pita.

An Appeal from the Publisher

Hello wonderful reader!

We hope you are enjoying this book.

We wanted to let you know that you have made an impact on many lives by reading this book.

Just to give you a brief introduction: We are a small publishing company with a team of 8 writers and 2 editors.

Most of our employees come from financially weaker section and our company is the only means they support their families. This is our way of giving back to the society.

We don't have the giant advertising budgets that many other publishers and businesses do online.

So, one way that you can really support our mission and our business is by leaving us a review on this book.

For a small company like us, getting reviews (especially on Amazon) means we can submit our books for advertising.

This means we can actually sell a few copies from time to time and make a bigger impact on the society as a whole. So, every review means a lot to us.

We can't THANK YOU enough for this!

SMASHED EGG TOASTS WITH HERBY LEMON YOGURT

Serving size: 4
Servings per recipe: 4
Calories: 437
Preparation time: 5 minutes
Cooking time: 15 minutes

Carbs: 7.4 g, Proteins: 23.5 g, Fats: 35.5 g

INGREDIENTS

- Large eggs - 8
- Garlic - 1 clove
- Medium lemon - 1
- Finely chopped fresh basil leaves, plus more for garnish - 2 tbsp
- Finely chopped fresh dill, plus more for garnish - 2 tbsp
- Finely chopped fresh chives, plus more for garnish - 2 tbsp

INGREDIENTS

- Plain Greek yogurt - 2 cups
- Extra-virgin olive oil, plus more for drizzling - 2 tbsp
- Kosher salt, plus more for sprinkling - ¾ tsp
- Freshly ground black pepper, plus more for sprinkling - ½ tsp
- Country or sourdough bread (about 1 inch thick) - 4 large slices
- Unsalted butter, divided - 4 tbsp

DIRECTIONS

1. Fill ¼ of a large pan with water and boil on high flame. Fill another large bowl with ice and cold water. Lower heat to simmer. Lower 8 eggs gently into the water, one at a time. Boil for 6.30 minutes. Now transfer eggs to the ice bath, after 2 minutes, peel eggs under running water.

2. Grate the zest of 1 medium-sized lemon finely. Squeeze and extract the juice. Mince garlic clove. Chop basil leaf to get 2 tbsp of leaves and the same amount of fresh dill and fresh chives. Add 2 cups yogurt (Greek) and 2 tbsp extra-virgin olive oil, ¾ tsp kosher salt, and ½ tsp black pepper. Whisk to combine.

3. Cut 4 slices (1-inch) of crusty bread. Melt 2 tbsp unsalted butter in a skillet of large size on medium flame. Add 2 slices. Cook until crisp and golden brown. Move to a large platter.

4. On bread slices, spread yogurt mixture and top with 2 eggs. With the back of a spoon, gently smash eggs. Spatter black pepper, kosher salt, and herbs. You can sprinkle a little more olive oil.

SPINACH AND ARTICHOKE FRITTATA

Serving size: 4
Servings per recipe: 2
Calories: 316
Preparation time: 5 minutes
Cooking time: 22 – 25 minutes

Carbs: 6.4 g Proteins: 17.9 g Fats: 25.9 g

INGREDIENTS

- 10 large eggs
- Full-fat sour cream - ½ cup
- Dijon mustard - 1 tbsp
- Kosher salt - 1 tsp
- Freshly ground black pepper - ¼ tsp
- Grated Parmesan cheese (about 3 oz.), divided - 1 cup
- Olive oil - 2 tbsp
- Marinated artichoke hearts, drained, patted dry, and quartered about 14 oz.
- Baby spinach - 5 oz.
- 2 cloves minced garlic

DIRECTIONS

1. Place a rack in the center of the oven and set the temperature to 400°c.
2. In a large bowl, put sour cream, mustard, pepper salt, and a half cup of Parmesan cheese. Stir with a whisk until well combined. Set aside.
3. Take a skillet of about 10 inches (non-stick or cast iron) and heat oil over medium flame. Put artichoke in a layer. Cook, stirring in between, until light brown, not more than 8 minutes. Now spinach and garlic are to be added. Toss until liquid evaporates.
4. After spreading the mixture evenly in a layer, pour the egg mixture over the vegetables. Sprinkle ½ cup of Parmesan. To set the eggs well over veggies, tilt it. Cook for 2-3 minutes or until the eggs settle.
5. Bake for 13-15 minutes. Cut in the center of the frittata to check for even cooking. Leave it for 5 minutes to cool, then slice into wedges.

SPINACH FETA BREAKFAST WRAPS

Serving size: 4
Servings per recipe: 4
Calories: 543
Preparation time: 10 minutes
Cooking time: 12 minutes

Carbs: 46.5 g Proteins: 28.1 g Fats: 27 g

INGREDIENTS

- Large eggs - 10
- Baby spinach - ½ lb
- Whole-wheat tortillas - 4
- Cherry or grape tomatoes, halved - ½ pint
- Feta cheese, crumbled - 4 oz.
- Butter or olive oil
- Salt
- Pepper

DIRECTIONS

1. Stir the eggs well to combine the white and yolks. Coat skillet's bottom with 1 tsp of olive oil and place on medium flame. When the butter melts or oil heats, drain the eggs in the skillet, stirring in between until the eggs are cooked. Add a pinch of salt with black pepper. Slide the material to a platter and cool at room temperature.

2. Rinse the skillet. Now put it on medium flame, and add another teaspoon of oil or butter. Add spinach. Keep stirring until the spinach is wilted. Spread wilted spinach on a plate and cool it to room temperature.

3. On a surface, arrange a tortilla. Add spinach, tomatoes, feta, and ¼ of the eggs in the middle of the tortilla and wrap tightly. Repeat the same procedure with the rest of the tortillas. In a gallon zip-top bag, place the wraps and freeze until ready to eat.

4. If you want to freeze longer than a week, wrap the burritos in aluminum foil, which will prevent freezer burn. Reheat in microwave on high for 2 minutes.

LUNCH
RECIPES

COLD LEMON ZOODLES

Serving size: 1
Servings per recipe: 4
Calories: 198
Preparation time: 20 minutes
Cooking time: 0 minute

Carbs: 8 g Proteins: 2 g Fats: 19 g

INGREDIENTS

- Zested and juiced lemon - 1
- Dijon mustard - ½ tsp
- Garlic powder - ½ tsp
- Olive oil - ⅓ cup
- Salt and freshly ground black pepper to taste
- Medium zucchini cut into noodles - 3
- Thinly sliced radishes - 1 bunch
- Chopped fresh thyme - 1 tbsp

DIRECTIONS

1. Whisk lemon zest, mustard, lemon juice, and garlic powder in a small bowl to combine.
2. Slowly add olive oil and whisk it to combine. Flavor with pepper and salt.
3. Toss zucchini noodles with radishes in a large bowl. After adding the dressing, toss until the veggies are well-coated.
4. Dress with fresh thyme and serve at once.

EGGPLANT AND HERB FLATBREAD

Serving size: 2
Servings per recipe: 8
Calories: 297
Preparation time: 5 minute
Cooking time: 1 hour

Carbs: 31 g Proteins: 15 g Fats: 12 g

INGREDIENTS

- Eggplants - 2 lbs
- Garlic cloves 6
- Ground cumin - ¼ tsp
- Paprika - ¼ tsp
- Olive oil - 2 tbsp
- Lemon juice - 1 tbsp
- Tahini - ¼ cup
- Kosher salt to taste

INGREDIENTS

- Eggplants - 2 lbs
- Garlic cloves 6
- Ground cumin - ¼ tsp
- Paprika - ¼ tsp
- Olive oil - 2 tbsp
- Lemon juice - 1 tbsp
- Tahini - ¼ cup
- Kosher salt to taste

- For the Flatbread
- Pizza dough - ½ lb (whole-wheat)
- Scallions sliced on a hard angle - 1 bunch
- Mint parsley and basil leaves - 1 large handful
- Lemon juice - 1 tbsp
- Kosher salt and freshly cracked black pepper to taste
- Olive oil
- Feta crumbled - ½ cup

DIRECTIONS

1.	With a fork, prick the eggplant all over. In the broiler, roast them until the skin is blackened all over and the eggplant is soft. Keep in a bowl and cover with plastic wrap. Set aside to cool for around 45 minutes.
2.	Remove the skin of the eggplant and cut the inside. Discard the skin and keep it in a tidy large bowl.
3.	Mince garlic finely; add a little salt while mincing to combine. Add the eggplant. Now add olive oil, cumin, paprika, and lemon juice. Stir to combine. Put the tahini, stir to combine. Check the taste and add salt and lemon juice as required.
4.	Preheat oven to 450°F.
5.	Roll the dough into a rectangle about the size of a sheet pan on a lightly floured surface. Move to an oiled baking sheet and mizzle with olive oil. Bake until it turns golden. After removing from the oven, apply a thick layer of eggplant mixture.
6.	Combine mint, scallions, parsley, and basil in a small bowl. Toss with salt, pepper, and lemon juice. Drizzle with olive oil and toss. Now put the mixture of herbs over the layer of eggplant. Give a finishing touch with feta. Serve at once.

EGGPLANT PIZZA

Serving Size: 1
Servings per recipe: 6
Calories: 257
Preparation time: 15 minutes
Cooking time: 20 minutes

Carbs: 13 g Proteins: 8 g Fats: 20 g

INGREDIENTS

- Eggplants - 1 large or 2 medium
- Olive oil - ⅓ cup
- Salt and freshly ground black pepper to taste
- Marinara sauce homemade - 1¼ cups
- Shredded mozzarella cheese - 1½ cups
- Cherry tomatoes, halved - 2 cups
- Basil leaves - ½ cup

DIRECTIONS

1. Preheat oven to 400°F. With parchment paper, line a baking sheet.
2. Slice the ends of the eggplant(s) and then cut into ¾-inch-thick slices. Set these slices on the readied baking sheets. Brush both sides of the slices with olive oil. Flavor with pepper and salt.
3. Roast slices of eggplant until almost tender (10-12 minutes).
4. Take the trays out from the oven and spread marinara sauce on top of each piece.
5. Place the pizza in the oven. Roast until the cheese melts and tomatoes get blistered (5-7 minutes).
6. Garnish pizza with basil and serve hot.

FIVE-MINUTE HEIRLOOM TOMATO TOAST

Serving size: 2
Servings per recipe: 3
Calories: 177
Preparation time: 5 minutes
Cooking time: 10 minutes

Carbs: 24 g Proteins: 3 g Fats: 8 g

INGREDIENTS

- Small heirloom tomato, diced - 1
- Persian cucumber, diced- 1
- Olive oil (extra-virgin) - 1 tsp
- Dried oregano pinch
- Freshly ground black pepper and kosher salt as per taste
- Low-fat whipped cream cheese - 2 tsp
- Trader Joe's Whole Grain Crisp bread - 2 pieces
- Balsamic glaze - 1 tsp

DIRECTIONS

1. Combine cucumber, olive oil, tomato, and oregano in a medium-sized bowl. Flavor with salt and pepper.
2. On the bread top, apply the cream cheese. Top it with a mixture of tomato and cucumber as well as the balsamic glaze.

GREEK LEMON CHICKEN SKEWERS WITH TZATZIKI SAUCE

Serving size: 1
Servings per recipe: 6
Calories: 68
Preparation time: 30 minutes
Cooking time: 1 hour

Carbs: 3 g Proteins: 4 g Fats: 5 g

INGREDIENTS

GREEK LEMON CHICKEN SKEWERS:

- 1 1/2 pounds boneless skinless chicken breasts, cut into approximately 1-inch cubes
- Fresh lemon juice - 3 tbsp.
- Red wine vinegar - 1 tbsp.
- Extra virgin olive oil - 1 tbsp.
- Garlic, 2 cloves (minced)
- Dried oregano - 2 tsp.

INGREDIENTS

- Dried parsley - 1/2 tsp.
- Coriander - 1/2 tsp.
- Kosher salt - 3/4 tsp
- Black pepper - 1/8 tsp.

TZATZIKI SAUCE:

- Greek yogurt - 1 cup
- Diced European cucumber - ½
- Extra-virgin olive oil - 1 tbsp
- Lemon juice - 2 tbsp
- Garlic powder pinch
- Salt and freshly ground black pepper to taste
- Fresh chopped dill - ¼ cup

GREEK LEMON CHICKEN SKEWERS

1. Mix yogurt, olive oil, cucumber, lemon juice, and garlic powder in a medium-sized bowl. Flavor with pepper and salt.
2. Whisk yogurt with lemon zest, lemon juice, oregano, cayenne, and garlic powder in a small bowl.
3. Rub the chicken with the yogurt-lemon mixture to coat well in a separate bowl.
4. Cover the chicken and refrigerate it for 45 minutes.
5. On each skewer, put one piece of chicken. Weave the strip back and forth while threading it onto the skewer to secure it.
6. With olive oil, brush both sides of skewers and then flavor with pepper and salt. In batches, cook on preheated grill or grill pan. Char nicely on both sides, for 4-5 minutes on each side.
7. Garnish with tzatziki sauce and parsley. Serve at once.

TZATZIKI SAUCE

1. Combine the ingredients (except the cucumber) in a medium-sized bowl and whisk together.
2. Stir in the cucumber and refrigerate until ready to serve.

GREEK LEMON CHICKEN SOUP

Serving size: 1
Servings per recipe: 4
Calories: 252.8
Preparation time: 10
Cooking time: 20

Carbs: 30.7 g Proteins: 24.8 g Fats: 4.4 g

INGREDIENTS

- Olive oil, divided - 2 tbsp
- Boneless, skinless chicken thighs, cut into 1-inch chunks - 1 lb
- Kosher salt and freshly ground black pepper to taste
- Minced garlic cloves - 4
- Diced onion - 1
- Peeled and diced carrots - 3
- Diced stalks celery - 2

INGREDIENTS

- Dried thyme - ½ tsp
- Chicken stock 8 cups
- Bay leaves - 2
- Cannellini beans, rinsed and drained - 15.5 ounce
- Baby spinach - 4 cups
- Freshly squeezed lemon juice, or more, to taste - 2 tbsp
- Chopped fresh parsley leaves - 2 tbsp
- Chopped fresh dill - 2 tbsp

DIRECTIONS

1. In a large stockpot or Dutch oven, heat 1 tbsp olive oil over medium flame.
    Flavor chicken thighs with pepper and salt as per your taste. Put the chicken in the
    stockpot. Keep cooking until golden (2-3 minutes). Set aside.
2. Now add 1 tbsp to stockpot. Add onion, carrots, celery, and garlic. Keep cooking
    until soft, stirring in between. Mix thyme until aromatic (1 minute).
3. Whisk in bay leaves and chicken stock. Bring to a boil. Lower heat. Stir chicken
    and cannellini beans. Mix occasionally, until slightly thick (10-15 minutes).
4. Now stir spinach to the point of wilting (for 2 minutes). Mix in parsley, dill, and
    lemon juice. Flavor with pepper and salt as per your taste. Serve at once.

GREEK MEATBALL MEZZE BOWLS

Serving size: 1½ cups
Serving per recipe: 4
Calories: 392
Preparation time: 10 minutes
Cooking time: 35 minutes

Carbs: 29.3 Proteins: 32.4 Fats: 17.2

INGREDIENTS

- Frozen chopped spinach, thawed - 1 cup
- 93% lean ground turkey - 1 lb
- Crumbled feta cheese - ½ cup
- Garlic powder - ½ tsp
- Dried oregano - ½ tsp
- Salt, divided - ⅜ tsp
- Ground pepper, divided - ⅜ tsp
- Cooked quinoa, cooled - 2 cups
- Lemon juice - 2 tbsp
- Olive oil - 1 tbsp
- Chopped parsley - ½ cup
- Chopped mint - 3 tbsp
- Sliced cucumber - 2 cups
- Cherry tomatoes - 1 pint
- Tzatziki - ¼ cup

DIRECTIONS

1. First, squeeze excess moisture from spinach. In a medium bowl, by mixing well, combine the spinach with turkey, feta, garlic powder, oregano, 1/8 tsp salt, and 1/8 tsp pepper. Prepare mixture into 12 meatballs. Over medium flame, place a large non-stick skillet. Coat it with spray. Now add meatballs to the pan and keep cooking until evenly brown and no longer pink in the center. It will take 10-12 minutes. Set the meatballs aside to cool.

2. Now, in a medium bowl, combine quinoa, lemon juice, oil, parsley, mint, and the remaining ¼ tsp salt and pepper each. Each is to be topped with 3 meatballs, ½ cup cucumbers, and ½ cup cherry tomatoes.

3. After this, seal the containers and refrigerate for up to 4 days. Now divide tzatziki into 4 small containers and put them in the fridge.

4. Before you serve, move the meatballs to a microwave-safe container and heat until steaming. Place back in the original container and serve with tzatziki.

GREEK YOGURT CHICKEN SALAD STUFFED PEPPERS

Serving size: 1
Servings per recipe: 6
Calories: 116
Preparation time: 30 minutes
Cooking time: 0 minute

Carbs: 16 g Proteins: 7 g Fats: 3 g

INGREDIENTS

- Greek yogurt - ⅔ cup
- Dijon mustard - 2 tbsp
- Seasoned rice vinegar - 2 tbsp
- Kosher salt and freshly ground black pepper
- Chopped fresh parsley - ⅓ cup
- Rotisserie chicken, cubed 1
- Sliced stalks celery - 4
- Sliced and divided scallions - 1 bunch
- Quartered and divided cherry tomatoes, - 1 pint
- Diced English cucumber - ½
- Halved and seeds-removed bell peppers - 3

DIRECTIONS

1. Whisk Greek yogurt, mustard, and rice vinegar in a medium-sized bowl. Flavor with pepper and salt. Stir in parsley.
2. Add celery, chicken, and three-quarters of tomatoes, scallions, and cucumber. Mix well to combine.
3. Among the bell pepper boats, divide chicken salad.
4. Dress with remaining tomatoes, scallions, and cucumber.

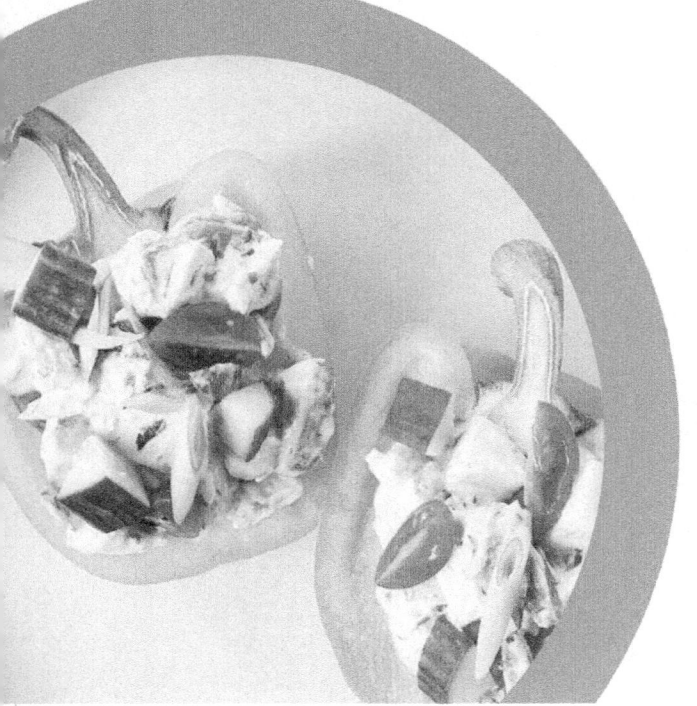

HARISSA POTATO SALAD

Serving size: 1
Servings per recipe: 4
Calories: 231
Preparation time: 10 minutes
Cooking time: 15 minutes

Carbs: 28 g Proteins: 3 g Fats: 12 g

INGREDIENTS

- Baby potatoes (leave the skins on) - 1½ lbs
- Harissa paste - 2 tbsp
- Low-fat or non-fat Greek yogurt - 6 oz.
- Salt - ¼ tsp
- Pepper - ¼ tsp
- Juice - 1 lemon
- Finely diced red onion - ¼ cup
- Fresh cilantro or parsley, roughly chopped - ¼ cup

DIRECTIONS

1. In a big pot, place potatoes. Cover and add 2 inches of salted cold water. Bring it to boil on medium flame. Keep cooking potatoes until fork tender (9-11 minutes). Drain water and set it aside to cool a bit.
2. Whisk harissa, salt, pepper, Greek yogurt, and lemon juice in a small bowl.
3. Move the potatoes to a large bowl. Add dressing. Gently fold it in until potatoes are well coated. Then carefully fold in herbs and diced red onion.
4. Serve at once, warm at room temperature, or when chilled.

MEDITERRANEAN BENTO LUNCH

Serving size: 1 bento box
Servings per recipe: 1
Calories: 497
Preparation time: 5 minutes
Cooking time: 15 minutes

Carbs: 60. 5 g Proteins: 36.7 g Fats: 13.8 g

INGREDIENTS

- Chickpeas, rinsed - ¼ cup
- Diced cucumber - ¼ cup
- Diced tomato - ¼ cup
- Diced olives - 1 tbsp
- Crumbled feta cheese- 1 tbsp
- Chopped fresh parsley - 1 tbsp
- Extra-virgin olive oil - ½ tsp
- Red-wine vinegar - 1 tsp
- Grilled turkey breast tenderloin or chicken breast - 3 oz.
- Grapes - 1 cup
- Whole-wheat pita bread, quartered - 1
- Hummus - 2 tbsp

DIRECTIONS

1. In a medium bowl, toss tomato, cucumber, chickpeas, feta, parsley, oil, olives, and vinegar. Pack this in a medium-sized container.
2. In a medium container, place turkey or chicken.
3. Pack hummus in a dip-size container and grapes and pita in small containers.

MEDITERRANEAN CHICKEN WITH ORZO SALAD

Serving size: ½ chicken breast and 1 cup orzo salad
Serving per recipe: 4
Calories: 402
Preparation time: 10 minutes
Cooking time: 40 minutes

Carbs: 28.3 g Proteins: 32 g Fats: 27.5 g

INGREDIENTS

- Skinless, boneless chicken breasts - (8 oz. each), halved 2
- Extra-virgin olive oil, divided - 3 tbsp
- Lemon zest - 1 tsp
- Salt, divided - ½ tsp
- Ground pepper, divided - ½ tsp
- Whole-wheat orzo - ¾ cup
- Thinly sliced baby spinach - 2 cups
- Chopped cucumber - 1 cup
- Chopped tomato - 1 cup
- Chopped red onion - ¼ cup
- Crumbled feta cheese ¼ cup
- Chopped Kalamata olives - 2 tbsp
- Lemon juice - 2 tbsp
- Garlic clove, grated- 1
- Chopped fresh oregano - 2 tsp

DIRECTIONS

1. Preheat oven to 425°F.
2. First, brush chicken with 1 tbsp oil and sprinkle with lemon zest, ¼ tsp salt, and 1 tsp pepper. Put it in a baking dish. Keep baking until an instant-read thermometer after insertion shows 165°F, or for 25-30 minutes.
3. Bring 32 oz. of water to a boil in a medium saucepan over a high flame. After this, add orzo and cook for 8 minutes. Now add spinach and cook for a minute. Drain and wash with cold water. Drain well and move to a large bowl. Add tomato, cucumber, onion, olives, and feta. Stir to combine.
4. In a small bowl, whisk the remaining 2 tbsp oil, garlic, lemon juice, oregano, and the remaining ¼ tsp salt and pepper each. Now stir everything except 1 tbsp of the dressing over the chicken. Serve it with salad.

MEDITERRANEAN CHICKPEA QUINOA BOWL

Serving size: 1
Servings per recipe: 4
Calories: 479
Preparation time: 5 minutes
Cooking time: 20 minutes

Carbs: 49.5 g Proteins: 12.7 g Fats: 24.8 g

INGREDIENTS

- Jar roasted red peppers, rinsed - 1 (7 oz.)
- Slivered almonds - ¼ cup
- Extra-virgin olive oil, divided - 4 tbsp
- Garlic, minced - 1 small clove
- Paprika - 1 tsp
- Ground cumin - ½ tsp
- Crushed red pepper - ¼ tsp (optional)
- Cooked quinoa - 2 cups
- Kalamata olives, chopped - ¼ cup
- Finely chopped red onion - ¼ cup
- Chickpeas, rinsed - 15 oz.
- Diced cucumber - 1 cup
- Crumbled feta cheese - ¼ cup
- Finely chopped fresh parsley - 2 tbsp

DIRECTIONS

1. In a mini food processor, place garlic, paprika, almonds, 2 tbsp oil, cumin, and crushed red pepper. Keep blending until smooth.

2. In a medium bowl, combine olives, red onion, quinoa, and the remaining 2 tbsp oil.

3. At the time of serving, divide quinoa mix into 4 bowls and top each with the same amount of cucumber, chickpeas, and red pepper sauce. Add parsley and feta.

PESTO QUINOA BOWLS WITH ROASTED VEGGIES AND LABNEH

Serving size: 1
Servings per recipe: 4
Calories: 862
Preparation time: 10 minutes
Cooking time: 40 minutes

Carbs: 96 g Proteins: 32 g Fats: 42 g

INGREDIENTS

- Large Japanese eggplant, cubed - 1
- Medium zucchini, cubed - 1
- Cherry tomatoes, sliced in half - 1 pint
- Romano (or green) beans - a handful
- Extra-virgin olive oil
- Kosher salt and freshly ground black pepper to taste
- Quinoa, rinsed - 1 cup
- Pesto ½ cup (homemade)
- Labneh or Greek yogurt - 1 cup
- Minced garlic clove - 1
- Juice from - ½ lemon
- Cilantro or parsley (or both!), roughly chopped handful

DIRECTIONS

1. Preheat oven to 400°F. With parchment paper, line a large baking sheet. Set up zucchini, eggplant, cherry tomatoes, and beans on it. Drizzle olive oil over the vegetables and flavor with pepper and salt. Keep roasting until all the vegetables turn tender or get caramelized. It generally takes 30-40 minutes.
2. Put quinoa in a medium-sized saucepan along with 2 cups of water and a little salt. Bring it to a boil. Cover it with a lid. Reduce flame to simmer and cook for around 15 minutes. After quinoa gets cooked, remove the lid. Fluff it with a fork and allow it to cool. After quinoa is cooled a bit, toss it using a pesto.
3. In a small bowl, mix garlic, lemon juice, herbs, and labneh.
4. Set up each bowl by placing quinoa and arranging veggies in a row to give a rainbow-like look. Then add a dollop of labneh on one side.

TOMATO SALAD WITH GRILLED HALLOUMI AND HERBS

Serving size: 1
Servings per recipe: 4 servings
Calories: 197
Preparation time: 8 minutes
Cooking time: 2 minutes

Carbs: 8 g Proteins: 9 g Fats: 15 g

INGREDIENTS

- Tomatoes, sliced into rounds - 1 lb
- Lemon - ½
- Flaky salt and freshly ground pepper
- Extra-virgin olive oil
- Halloumi cheese, sliced into 4 slabs - ½ lb
- Basil leaves, torn - 5
- Finely chopped flat-leaf parsley - 2 tbsp

DIRECTIONS

1. On a medium-high flame, pre-heat a grill or grill pan.
2. On a serving plate, arrange tomatoes. Squeeze lemon lightly over them. Flavor with pepper and flaky salt.
3. Oil the grill grates and add halloumi. Cook, turning once or until marks of grill appear and cheese is thoroughly warmed. It generally takes 1 minute per side. Moisten salad with olive oil. Dot with parsley and basil. Serve at once.

WILD ALASKA SALMON AND SMASHED CUCUMBER GRAIN BOWLS

Serving size: 1
Servings per recipe: 4
Calories: 841
Preparation time: 15 minutes
Cooking time: 40 minutes

Carbs: 69 g Proteins: 49 g Fats: 43 g

INGREDIENTS

- Farro - 2 cups
- Juice of - 2 lemons
- Dijon mustard - 2 tbsp
- Minced garlic clove - 1
- Extra-virgin olive oil - ⅓ cup plus 2 tbsp
- Kosher salt and freshly ground black pepper to taste
- European cucumber, cut into 1-inch chunks - 1
- Seasoned rice vinegar - ¼ cup
- Chopped fresh parsley - ¼ cup
- Chopped fresh mint - ¼ cup
- Chopped fresh dill - ¼ cup
- Four wild Alaska sockeye salmon fillets - 6-ounce

DIRECTIONS

1. Bring a large pot of salted water to boil. Put farro into boiling water. Cook until wilted (25-30 minutes). Drain.

2. In a medium bowl, add farro. Now mix mustard, garlic, lemon juice, and ⅓ cup of olive oil. Flavor with pepper and salt.

3. Roughly smash cucumber chunks with a large fork in a separate medium-sized bowl. After adding rice vinegar, toss to combine. Flavor with pepper and salt. Add mint, dill, and parsley.

4. Heat the remaining 2 tbsp olive oil in a skillet over medium heat. Flavor salmon with salt and pepper. Next, add fillets to hot oil and keep cooking until the desired level of doneness is attained or 8-10 minutes.

5. Now divide farro into 4 bowls. Break one salmon fillet in each bowl. Top with herbs and cucumbers.

15-MINUTE MEDITERRANEAN COUSCOUS WITH TUNA AND PEPPERONCINI

Serving size: 1
Servings per recipe: 4
Calories: 226
Preparation time: 3 minutes
Cooking time: 12 minutes

Carbs: 44 g Proteins: 8 g Fats: 1 g

INGREDIENTS

COUSCOUS
- Chicken broth or water - 1 cup
- Couscous - 1¼ cups
- Kosher salt - ¾ tsp
- Accompaniments
- Tuna - two
- 5-ounce oil-packed cans
- Cherry tomatoes, halved - 1 pint
- Sliced pepperoncini - ½ cup
- Chopped fresh parsley - ⅓ cup
- Capers - ¼ cup
- Olive oil (extra-virgin) for serving
- Freshly ground black pepper and kosher salt to taste
- Quartered lemon - 1

DIRECTIONS

1. Bring water or broth to boil in a small pot on medium flame. Take the pot off the pot, stir the couscous, and cover the pot with a lid. Leave for 10 minutes.
2. Toss together tomatoes, tuna, pepperoncini, capers, and parsley.
3. With a fork, fluff the couscous. Flavor with pepper and salt, and mizzle with olive oil. With a tuna mixture, top the couscous. Your dish is ready to be served with lemon wedges.

15-MINUTE MEZZE PLATE WITH TOASTED ZA'ATAR PITA BREAD

Serving size: 1
Servings per recipe: 4
Calories: 731
Preparation time: 10 minutes
Cooking time: 5 minutes

Carbs: 62 g Proteins: 26 g Fats: 48 g

INGREDIENTS

- Whole-wheat pita rounds - 4
- Extra-virgin olive oil - 4 tbsp
- Za'atar - 4 tsp
- Greek yogurt 1 cup
- Kosher salt and freshly ground black pepper to taste
- Hummus - 1 cup
- Marinated artichoke hearts - 1 cup
- Sliced roasted red peppers - 1 cup
- Assorted olives - 2 cups
- Cherry tomatoes - 2 cups
- Salami - 4 oz

DIRECTIONS

1. Over medium flame, heat a large skillet. Each side of the pita is to be brushed with olive oil. Flavor it with zaátar.
2. Now work in parts. Add pita to the skillet and toast until it turns golden brown, for around 2 minutes on each side. Cut each pita into quarters.
3. With salt and pepper, flavor Greek yogurt.
4. To assemble, divide Greek yogurt, artichoke hearts, roasted red peppers, pitas, hummus, tomatoes, and salami among 4 plates.

DINNER
RECIPES

BAKED CHICKEN AND RICOTTA MEATBALLS

Serving size: 5 balls
Servings per recipe: 4
Calories: 454
Preparation time: 15 minutes
Cooking time: 20 minutes

Carbs: 20 g Proteins: 36 g Fats: 27 g

INGREDIENTS

- Broccolini, rough stems trimmed and thick pieces cut lengthwise - 14 oz. (400g)
- Lemon, ends trimmed and thinly sliced - 1
- Extra-virgin olive oil, divided - 4 tbsp
- Kosher salt and freshly ground black pepper to taste
- Crushed red pepper flakes - ½ tsp or more if desired

INGREDIENTS

- Large egg - 1
- Grated garlic cloves - 2
- Ricotta cheese, drained and lightly salted - ¾ cup
- Parsley leaves and fine stems, roughly chopped - ½ cup
- Panko breadcrumbs - ¾ cup
- Ground chicken, preferably dark meat - 1 lb
- Juice of 1 lemon
- Grated Parmesan, for sprinkling (optional)

DIRECTIONS

1. Preheat the oven to 425°F .
2. Toss the broccoli and lemon slices with 3 tbsp of olive oil, salt, red pepper flakes, and pepper on a baking sheet. Apply evenly on the baking sheet and set aside while meatballs are being made.
3. Beat the egg. Add the garlic, ricotta, 1 tsp salt, pepper, parsley, rest of the oil, breadcrumbs, and meat. Combine gently using your hands (too much mushing will make these items dry and tough). The pieces of meat should be visible through seasoning. Wet your hands lightly with water and oil and roll the meat into 20 loose, round shapes, a little smaller than golf balls. Use a smaller rolling motion between your hands. The water you used will keep them from sticking to your hands. Place large pieces of baking parchment on the counter to make it easy for you to clean.
4. On the baking sheet, nestle the meatballs between the broccoli and lemon. Keep baking until the meatballs are brown and cooked through and the broccoli becomes crispy. It generally takes 15-20 minutes. Shake the baking sheet to move the meatballs and turn the tray around midway to make sure that it gets evenly cooked.
5. Take it out of the oven, squeeze the lemon juice on top, and place it on the plates. Give it a finishing touch with grated Parmesan.

BBQ SHRIMP WITH GARLICKY KALE AND PARMESAN-HERB COUSCOUS

Serving size: 3 oz. shrimp, 1 cup kale, and ½ cup couscous
Servings per recipe: 4
Calories: 414
Preparation time: 10 minutes
Cooking time: 20 minutes

Carbs: 36.4 g Proteins: 32.4 g Fats: 16.9 g

INGREDIENTS

- Low-sodium chicken broth - 1 cup
- Poultry seasoning - ¼ tsp
- Whole-wheat couscous - ⅔ cup
- Grated Parmesan cheese - ⅓ cup
- Butter - 1 tbsp
- Extra-virgin olive oil, divided - 3 tbsp
- Chopped kale - 8 cups
- Water - ¼ cup
- Smashed garlic clove - 1 large
- Crushed red pepper - ¼ tsp
- Salt - ¼ tsp
- Peeled and deveined raw shrimp - 1 lb (26-30 per lb)
- Barbecue sauce - ¼ cup

DIRECTIONS

1. In a medium-size saucepan, combine broth and poultry over medium heat. Bring to a boil and stir in couscous. Remove from flame and cover the pan. Leave it for around 5 minutes. Fluff with a fork, then stir in Parmesan and butter. Keep it covered so that it stays warm longer.

2. In a large skillet, heat 1 tbsp oil on medium heat. Add kale and cook for 1-2 minutes or until it looks bright green. Now pour water. Cover the skillet and cook, stirring until kale is soft, for about 3 minutes. Bring heat down to medium-low. Dig in the center of kale and add 1 tbsp oil, garlic, and crushed red pepper. Cook, constantly, for 15 seconds. Then stir the garlic oil into kale and flavor with salt. Move to a bowl and cover to keep it warm.

3. Now put 1 tbsp oil and shrimp into the pan. Keep cooking, stirring in between until the shrimp is curled and pink (2 minutes) Remove from the flame and stir in barbecue sauce. Serve the shrimp with couscous and kale.

BROCCOLI RABE AND BURRATA WITH LEMON

Serving size: 1
Servings per recipe: 4
Calories: 198
Preparation time: 2 minutes
Cooking time: 8 minutes

Carbs: 6 g Proteins: 11 g Fats: 15 g

INGREDIENTS

- Broccoli rabe, tips of stems trimmed off - 1 bunch
- Extra-virgin olive oil, plus more for drizzling - 1 to 2 tbsp
- Sliced garlic cloves - 2
- Red-pepper flakes - ¼ tsp
- Burrata or fresh mozzarella - 4 oz.
- Fresh lemon juice - ½ tbsp
- Crushed, toasted pistachios - 2 tbsp
- Flaky sea salt, for serving

DIRECTIONS

1. In a large pot, bring salted water to a boil. For 3 minutes, boil the broccoli rabe, then drain.
2. Heat 1-2 tbsp of olive oil in a large, deep skillet over medium heat. It should cover the bottom of the pan nicely. First, stir in garlic and cook for 30 seconds. Then stir in the red pepper flakes.
3. In the pan, add the broccoli and sauté, shaking the pan and gently tossing it so that cooking gets done, until tender (especially the stems), 3-5 minutes.
4. Take the broccoli rabe from the pan and drain off any excess liquid. On a plate, arrange broccoli. Tear the burrata and scatter the pieces among the broccoli rabe. Sprinkle lemon juice, pistachios, and salt. Drizzle with olive oil, if you wish. Your dish is ready to be served.

CHARRED SHRIMP AND PESTO BUDDHA BOWLS

Serving size: 1½ cups
Servings per recipe: 4
Calories: 429
Preparation time: 5 minutes
Cooking time: 20 minutes

Carbs: 29.3 g Proteins: 30.9 g Fats: 22 g

INGREDIENTS

- Prepared pesto - ⅓ cup
- Balsamic vinegar - 2 tbsp
- Extra-virgin olive oil - 1 tbsp
- Salt - ½ tsp
- Ground pepper - ¼ tsp
- Peeled and deveined large shrimp, patted dry - 1 lb (16-20 count)
- Arugula - 4 cups
- Cooked quinoa - 2 cups
- Halved cherry tomatoes - 1 cup
- Diced avocado - 1

DIRECTIONS

1. In a large bowl, whisk vinegar, pesto, oil, pepper, and salt. Remove 4 tbsp of mixture. Set both bowls aside.
2. Over medium flame, heat a large cast-iron skillet. Add shrimp and cook, stirring until the shrimp is cooked through and slightly charred (4-5 minutes). Transfer to a plate.
3. In a large bowl, add quinoa and arugula with vinaigrette and toss to coat. Divide the arugula mixture between 4 bowls. Top with tomatoes, avocado, and shrimp. Drizzle each bowl with 1 tbsp of the reserved pesto mixture.

CHICKEN AND SPINACH SKILLET PASTA WITH LEMON AND PARMESAN

Serving size: Scant 2 cups
Servings per recipe: 4
Calories: 335
Preparation time: 10 minutes
Cooking time: 25 minutes

Carbs: 24.9 g Proteins: 28.7 g Fats: 12.3 g

INGREDIENTS

- Gluten-free whole-wheat penne pasta - 8 oz.
- Extra-virgin olive oil - 2 tbsp
- Boneless, skinless chicken breast or thighs, trimmed, if necessary, and cut into bite-size pieces - 1 lb
- Salt - ½ tsp
- Ground pepper - ¼ tsp
- Garlic, minced - 4 cloves
- Dry white wine - ½ cup
- Juice and zest of - 1 lemon
- Chopped fresh spinach - 10 cups
- Grated Parmesan cheese, divided - 4 tbsp

DIRECTIONS

1. Follow the cooking directions given on the package to cook pasta.
2. In a large high-sided skillet, heat oil. Add chicken, pepper, and salt. Cook, stirring now and then, for 5-7 minutes. Now add garlic. Cook until aromatic, for about 1 minute. Stir in lemon juice, wine, and zest. Now bring it to a simmer.
3. Remove from flame. Stir in spinach and cooked pasta. Cover the skillet and leave it until the spinach is soft. Divide it among 4 plates and add toppings over each with 1 tbsp of Parmesan.

CHICKPEA VEGETABLE COCONUT CURRY

Serving size: 1
Servings per recipe: 4
Calories: 665
Preparation time: 10 minutes
Cooking time: 20 minutes

Carbs: 80 g Proteins 26 g Fats: 31 g

INGREDIENTS

- Extra-virgin olive oil - 1 tbsp
- Thinly sliced red onion - 1
- Thinly sliced red bell pepper - 1
- Minced fresh ginger - 1 tbsp
- Minced garlic cloves - 3
- Small head cauliflower, cut into bite-size florets - 1
- Chili powder - 2 tsp

INGREDIENTS

- Ground coriander - 1 tsp
- Red curry paste - 3 tbsp
- Coconut milk - 14 oz.
- Halved lime - 1
- Chickpeas - 28 oz.
- Frozen peas - 1½ cups
- Kosher salt and freshly ground black pepper to taste
- Steamed rice, for serving (optional)
- Chopped fresh cilantro - ¼ cup
- Thinly sliced scallions - 4

DIRECTIONS

1. Heat oil over medium flame in a large saucepan. Add onion and bell pepper. Sauté until almost tender, for about 5 minutes. Next, add garlic and ginger. Sauté until aromatic, for around 1 minute.
2. Add cauliflower. Toss well so as to combine. Stir in coriander, chili powder, and red curry paste. Cook until it starts becoming caramelized. It generally takes about a minute.
3. Stir in coconut milk and bring it to a simmer on medium-low flame. The saucepan should be covered while you continue to simmer until the cauliflower is tender. It will take 8-10 minutes.
4. Take off the lid and squeeze the lemon juice into the curry. Stir it well to combine. Now add chickpeas and peas. Flavor with pepper and salt. Next, bring it back to simmer.
5. It is recommended that you serve it with rice. Dress each portion with 1 tbsp of cilantro and 1 tbsp of scallions.

GREEK CAULIFLOWER RICE BOWLS WITH GRILLED CHICKEN

Serving size: 4
Servings per recipe: 2
Calories: 411
Preparation time: 5 minutes
Cooking time: 30 minutes

Carbs: 29 g Proteins: 9.5 g Fats: 27 g

INGREDIENTS

- Extra-virgin olive oil, divided 6 tbsp plus - 1 tsp
- Cauliflower rice - 4 cups
- Chopped red onion - ⅓ cup
- Salt, divided - ¾ tsp
- Chopped fresh dill, divided - ½ cup
- Boneless, skinless chicken breasts - 1 lb
- Ground pepper, divided - ½ tsp
- Lemon juice - 3 tbsp
- Dried oregano - 1 tsp
- Halved cherry tomatoes - 1 cup
- Chopped cucumber - 1 cup
- Chopped Kalamata olives - 2 tbsp
- Crumbled feta cheese - 2 tbsp
- Lemon wedges for serving - 4

DIRECTIONS

1. Preheat grill to medium.
2. Over a medium-high flame, heat 2 tbsp oil in a large skillet. Cook for about 5 minutes or until the cauliflower is softened. Stir occasionally. Remove from heat and mix in ¼ cup dill.
3. Rub 1 tsp oil all over the chicken. Sprinkle with ¼ tsp pepper and ¼ tsp salt. Flip and grill. Using an instant-read thermometer, check the thickest part of the breast. It should show a temperature of 165°F (15 minutes total). Cut in crosswise slices.
4. In a small bowl, whisk the remaining 4 tbsp oil, lemon juice, oregano, and ¼ tsp salt and pepper.
5. Divide the cauliflower rice among 4 bowls. Top with tomatoes, cucumber, chicken, olives, and feta. Sprinkle with remaining ¼ cup dill. Drizzle vinaigrette. You can serve with lemon wedges.

GREEN SHAKSHUKA WITH SPINACH, CHARD, AND FETA

Serving size: 1 egg and ½ cup greens
Servings per recipe: 6
Calories: 296
Preparation time: 10 minutes
Cooking time: 20 minutes

Carbs: 8.5 g Proteins: 10.7 g Fats: 23.4 g

INGREDIENTS

- Extra-virgin olive oil - ⅓ cup
- Finely chopped large onion - 1
- Chard, stemmed and chopped - 12 oz.
- Mature spinach, stemmed and chopped - 12 oz.
- Dry white wine - ½ cup
- Small jalapeño or serrano pepper, thinly sliced - 1
- Cloves garlic, very thinly sliced - 2 medium
- Kosher salt - ¼ tsp
- Ground pepper - ¼ tsp
- Low-sodium no-chicken or chicken broth - ½ cup
- Unsalted butter - 2 tbsp
- Large eggs- 6
- Crumbled feta or goat cheese - ½ cup

DIRECTIONS

1. In a large skillet, heat oil over medium flame. Cook for 7-8 minutes, adding onion, stirring in between, until soft and translucent but not brown. Add spinach and chard a few handfuls at a time and cook, stirring often, until soft. Add wine garlic, jalapeno, garlic, pepper, and salt. Cook, stirring in between to the point that wine gets absorbed and the garlic turns soft. Add butter and broth. Cook, stirring to the point that the butter melts and liquid gets absorbed, 1 to 2 minutes.

2. Crack the eggs over the veggies. Cover the skillet and cook over medium-low flame until the whites are set (3-5 minutes). Remove from flame and dredge with cheese. Cover and leave for 2 minutes, then serve.

MEDITERRANEAN PORTOBELLO MUSHROOM PIZZAS WITH ARUGULA SALAD

Serving size: 1
Servings per recipe: 2
Calories: 264
Preparation time: 10 minutes
Cooking time: 35 minutes

Carbs: 25 g Proteins: 14 g Fats: 13 g

INGREDIENTS

- Large portobello mushroom caps - (about 4 oz. each), gills removed 8
- Olive oil 2 tbsp, divided - 1 tsp
- Ground pepper - ½ tsp
- Pizza or tomato sauce - ½ cup
- Lightly packed baby spinach, chopped - 2 cups
- Sun-dried chopped tomatoes - ½ cup (about 8)
- Rinsed and chopped artichoke hearts - 1 (14 oz.)
- Shredded part-skim mozzarella cheese - ½ cup
- Crumbled feta cheese - ¼ cup
- Dried Italian seasoning - ½ tsp.
- Lemon juice - 1 tbsp.
- Lightly packed baby arugula - 2 cups
- Fresh basil leaves (thinly sliced) - ¼ cup

DIRECTIONS

1. Preheat oven to 400°F. Use foil to line a large baking sheet and keep it on a wire rack. With 1 tbsp olive oil, brush tops of portobello caps. Now place them undersides-up on the rack. Roast for 10 minutes. Change sides and roast for another 5 minutes.
2. Take portobellos out from the oven and flip them carefully to bring the underside up. Flavor with ¼ tsp pepper. Apply 1 tbsp sauce inside each cap. Divide sun-dried tomatoes, mozzarella, and feta among caps. Sprinkle with Italian flavors. Now place portobellos in the oven again and bake to the point where the cheese melts and turns brown (10-15 minutes).
3. Whisk the remaining 1 tbsp pepper, 1 tsp oil, and 1/8 tsp pepper and lemon juice in a medium-sized bowl. Now add arugula and toss to coat.
4. Dress the portobello pizzas with basil and serve with arugula salad.

MEDITERRANEAN STUFFED CHICKEN BREASTS

Serving size: ½ breast
Servings per recipe: 8
Calories: 179
Preparation time: 35 minutes
Cooking time: 25 minutes

Carbs: 1.9 g Proteins: 24.4 g Fats: 7.4 g

INGREDIENTS

- Crumbled feta cheese - ½ cup
- Chopped roasted red bell peppers - ½ cup
- Chopped fresh spinach - ½ cup
- Kalamata olives, pitted and quartered - ¼ cup
- Chopped fresh basil - 1 tbsp
- Chopped fresh flat-leaf parsley - 1 tbsp
- Minced cloves garlic - 2
- Boneless, skinless chicken breasts - 4 (8-ounce)
- Salt - ¼ tsp
- Ground pepper - ½ tsp
- Extra-virgin olive oil - 1 tbsp
- Lemon juice - 1 tbsp

DIRECTIONS

1. Heat oven beforehand to 400°F. In a medium bowl, combine feta, spinach, roasted red peppers, olives, basil, parsley, and garlic.

2. To form a pocket, cut a horizontal slit through the thickest portion of each chicken breast. With ⅓ cup of feta mixture, stuff each breast pocket, using wooden picks to secure the pockets. With pepper and salt, sprinkle the chicken evenly.

3. In a large oven-safe skillet, heat oil over medium flame. Set stuffed breasts upside down in the pan. Cook until golden, about 2 minutes. Flip the chicken carefully. Move the pan to the oven. Keep baking until an instant-read thermometer is inserted in the thickest portion of the chicken and shows 165°F (20-25 minutes). Drizzle chicken evenly with lemon juice. Keep in mind to remove the wooden picks from the chicken before serving.

ONE-SKILLET SALMON WITH FENNEL AND SUN-DRIED TOMATO COUSCOUS

Serving size: 4 oz. salmon and 1¼ cups couscous
Servings per recipe: 4
Calories: 543
Preparation time: 10 minutes
Cooking time: 30 minutes

Carbs: 46 g Proteins: 38.3 g Fats: 7.6 g

INGREDIENTS

- Lemon - 1
- Salmon, skinned and cut into 4 portions - 1 ¼ lbs
- Salt - ¼ tsp
- Ground pepper - ¼ tsp
- Sun-dried tomato pesto, divided - 4 tbsp
- Extra-virgin olive oil, divided 2 tbsp
- Fennel bulbs, cut into ½-inch wedges; fronds reserved - 2 medium
- Israeli couscous, preferably whole-wheat - 1 cup
- Scallions, sliced - 3
- Low-sodium chicken broth- 1 ½ cups
- Sliced green olives - ¼ cup
- Toasted pine nuts - 2 tbsp
- Garlic, sliced - 2 cloves

DIRECTIONS

1. Grate lemon zest and preserve it. Slice 8 pieces of lemon. Flavor lemon with pepper and salt. Next, apply 1½ tsp of pesto to each piece.

2. In a large skillet, heat 1 tbsp oil over medium flame. For 2-3 minutes, cook half the fennel until it turns brown at the bottom. Turn the flame down and repeat with 1 tbsp oil and fennel. Move to the plate. In the pan, add scallions and couscous. Cook, stirring frequently, until the couscous turns lightly toasted (1-2 minutes). Stir in broth, pine nuts, olives, garlic, reserved zest, and leftover 2 tbsp of pesto.

3. Take the couscous and nestle fennel and salmon into it. Using lemon slices, top the salmon. Turn down the flame to medium-low. Cook, keeping the pan covered until the salmon is thoroughly cooked (10-15 minutes). Dress with fennel fronds if you wish to do so.

PROSCIUTTO PIZZA WITH CORN AND ARUGULA

Serving size: ¼ pizza
Servings per recipe: 4
Calories: 436
Preparation time: 10 minutes
Cooking time: 20 minutes

Carbs: 53.1 g Proteins: 18.3 g Fats: 19.9 g

INGREDIENTS

- Pizza dough, preferably whole-wheat - 1 lb
- Extra-virgin olive oil, divided - 2 tbsp
- Minced clove garlic - 1
- Part-skim shredded mozzarella cheese - 1 cup
- Fresh corn kernels - 1 cup
- Very thinly sliced prosciutto, torn into 1-inch pieces - 1 ounce
- Arugula - 1 ½ cups
- Torn fresh basil - ½ cup
- Ground pepper - ¼ tsp

DIRECTIONS

1. Preheat grill to medium-high flame.
2. On a lightly floured surface, roll dough into a 12-inch oval. Move it to a lightly floured baking sheet. In a small bowl, combine 1 tbsp oil and garlic. Bring the garlic oil, cheese, dough, corn, and prosciutto to the grill.
3. Apply oil to the grill rack. Move the crust to the grill. Keep grilling the dough until it gets puffed and turns slightly brown (1-2 minutes).
4. Turn the crust over and apply garlic oil to it. Top with corn, cheese, and prosciutto. Grill, covering it, until the cheese is melted and the crust is lightly brown at the bottom or 2-3 minutes more. Put the pizza back on the baking sheet.
5. Top the pizza with basil, arugula, and pepper. Drizzle with the leftover tablespoon of oil.

SHEET-PAN SALMON WITH SWEET POTATOES AND BROCCOLI

Serving size: 2
Servings per recipe: 4
Calories: 504
Preparation time: 15 minutes
Cooking time: 20 minutes

Carbs: 34 g Proteins: 34 g Fats: 26 g

INGREDIENTS

- Low-fat mayonnaise - 3 tbsp
- Chili powder - 1 tsp
- Medium sweet potatoes, peeled and cut into 1-inch cubes - 2
- Olive oil, divided - 4 tsp
- Salt, divided - ½ tsp
- Ground pepper, divided - ¼ tsp
- Broccoli florets - 4 cups (8 oz.; 1 medium crown)
- Salmon fillet, cut into - 4 portions - 1 ¼ lbs
- Limes 2 – 1 zested and juiced, 1 cut into wedges for serving
- Crumbled feta or cotija cheese - ¼ cup
- Chopped fresh cilantro - ½ cup

DIRECTIONS

1. Preheat the oven to 425°F. With a foil, line a large rimmed baking sheet and coat with cooking spray.

2. Combine chili powder and mayonnaise in a small bowl. Set aside.

3. In a medium bowl, toss sweet potatoes with 2 tsp oil, ¼ tsp salt, and 1/8 tsp pepper. Spread it on the prepared baking sheet. Roast it for 15 minutes.

4. In the same bowl, toss broccoli with the remaining 2 tsp oil, 1/8 tsp pepper, and ¼ tsp salt. Now remove the baking sheet from the oven. Stir the sweet potatoes and push them to the sides of the pan. Move salmon to the center of the pan and on either side spread broccoli, among sweet potatoes. Spread 2 tbsp of mayonnaise mixture over the salmon. Bake for around 15 minutes or until the sweet potatoes are tender and the salmon flakes easily with a fork.

5. Add lime zest and lemon juice to the remaining 1 tbsp of low-fat mayonnaise. Mix it well.

6. Among 4 plates, divide salmon and top with cheese and cilantro. Divide the broccoli and sweet potatoes among the plates. Drizzle with the lime-mayonnaise sauce. You can serve it with wedges of lime and any leftover sauce.

SLOW-COOKER MEDITERRANEAN QUINOA WITH ARUGULA

Serving size: 1½ cups
Servings per recipe: 6
Calories: 352
Preparation time: 25 minutes
Cooking time: 3-4 hours

Carbs: 46 g Proteins: 12 g Fats: 13 g

INGREDIENTS

- Unsalted vegetable stock - 2 ¼ cups
- Uncooked quinoa, rinsed - 1 ½ cups
- Sliced red onions- (from 1 onion) 1 cup
- Minced garlic cloves - 2 (about 2 tsp)
- No-salt-added chickpeas (garbanzo beans), drained and rinsed - 1 can (15.5 oz.)
- Olive oil - 2 ½ tbsp
- Kosher salt - ¾ tsp
- Fresh lemon juice (from one lemon) - 2 tsp
- Drained, chopped roasted red bell peppers (from the jar) - ½ cup
- Baby arugula - 4 cups (about 4 oz.)
- Feta cheese, crumbled - 2 oz. (about ½ cup)
- Kalamata olives, halved lengthwise - 12 pitted
- Coarsely chopped fresh oregano - 2 tbsp

DIRECTIONS

1. In a 5- to 6-quart slow cooker, stir stock, quinoa, garlic, chickpeas, onions, 1½ tsp of olive oil, and ½ tsp of salt.
2. Close the cooker lid and cook on low flame until the quinoa is soft and stock is absorbed (3-4 hours).
3. Turn off the slow cooker. With a fork, fluff the quinoa mixture.
4. Now mix lemon juice, the remaining 2 tbsp olive oil, and ¼ tsp salt with a whisker.
5. Put the red bell peppers and olive oil into a slow cooker.
6. Gently toss to combine and fold in the arugula in the same manner.
7. Keep it this way for 10 minutes or until the arugula is gently wilted.
8. Drizzle each serving evenly with feta cheese, olive oil, and oregano.

TOMATO POACHED COD WITH SPECIAL HERBS

Serving size: 1 bowl
Servings per recipe: 4
Calories: 261
Preparation time: 5 minutes
Cooking time: 25 minutes

Carbs: 19 g Proteins: 30 g Fats: 8 g

INGREDIENTS

- Extra-virgin olive oil - 2 tbsp
- Thinly sliced shallot - 1
- Kosher salt and freshly ground black pepper to taste
- Thinly sliced garlic clove - 1
- Crushed red pepper flakes, or more, as desired - ½ tsp
- Crushed tomatoes and their liquid - 14 oz.
- Low-sodium vegetable stock (or water) - 1 cup
- Cod fillets - 4, 5-ounce
- Parsley or basil leaves and fine stems, roughly chopped or torn, for sprinkling - 1 cup
- Toasted crusty bread, for serving

DIRECTIONS

1. In a wide, shallow skillet, heat oil until it is shimmering. Add salt and shallot, stirring until these get soft. Generally, it takes 3 minutes. Add pepper and garlic flakes. Keep stirring until aromatic, for about 30 seconds more. Pour in stock and tomatoes and turn the flame high. Bring the mixture to boil. Turn the flame down to simmer. Keep stirring in between. Flavor with salt and pepper. Allow it to cook until tomatoes are slightly liquid. It generally takes 8-10 minutes.

2. Flavor the fish with salt and pepper and add the sauce. Adjust the heat to maintain a gentle simmer. Cook and spoon the sauce over the fillets, until the fish is covered. It should flake easily when touched, after about 5 minutes. If these don't submerge fully, turn them over halfway. It may take a little longer to cook thick fillets.

3. Between the serving bowls, divide the fish. Put the sauce on top with a spoon. Give a finishing touch with pepper and parsley. It should be served with bread for dipping.

VEGAN MEDITERRANEAN LENTIL SOUP

Serving size: 1 cup
Servings per recipe: 6
Calories: 272
Preparation time: 20 minutes
Cooking time: 40 minutes

Carbs: 42 g Proteins: 13 g Fats: 7 g

INGREDIENTS

- Extra-virgin olive oil - 2 tbsp
- Chopped yellow onions - 1 ½ cups
- Chopped carrots - 1 cup
- Minced garlic - 3 cloves
- No-salt-added tomato paste - 2 tbsp
- Reduced-sodium vegetable broth - 4 cups
- Water - 1 cup
- No-salt-added cannellini beans, rinsed - 1 (15 oz.)
- Mixed dry lentils (brown, green, and black) - 1 cup
- Chopped sun-dried tomatoes in oil, drained - ½ cup
- Salt - ¾ tsp
- Ground pepper - ½ tsp
- Chopped fresh dill, plus more for garnish - 1 tbsp
- Red-wine vinegar - 1 ½ tsp

DIRECTIONS

1. In a large heavy pot, heat oil on medium flame. Add carrots and onion. Cook, stirring in between, until soft (3-4 minutes).
2. Next, add garlic and cook, stirring constantly, until the mixture is coated evenly, about 1 minute.
3. Stir in broth, water, cannellini beans, lentils, sun-dried tomatoes, salt, and pepper.
4. Bring to a boil over medium-high heat. Reduce heat to medium-low.
5. After covering, let it simmer until lentils turn soft, 30-40 minutes.
6. Remove from flame and stir in vinegar and dill. You can add additional dill as per your taste.

WALNUT-ROSEMARY CRUSTED SALMON

Serving size: 3 oz.
Servings per recipe: 4
Calories: 222
Preparation time: 10 minutes
Cooking time: 10 minutes

Carbs: 4 g Proteins: 24 g Fats: 12 g

INGREDIENTS

- Dijon mustard - 2 tsp
- Minced clove garlic - 1
- Lemon zest - ¼ tsp
- Lemon juice - 1 tsp
- Chopped fresh rosemary - 1 tsp
- Honey - ½ tsp
- Kosher salt - ½ tsp
- Crushed red pepper - ¼ tsp
- Panko breadcrumbs - 3 tbsp
- Finely chopped walnuts - 3 tbsp
- Extra-virgin olive oil - 1 tsp
- Skinless salmon fillet, fresh or frozen - 1 (1 lb)
- Olive oil cooking spray - 1 serving
- Chopped fresh parsley and lemon wedges for garnish

DIRECTIONS

1. Preheat oven to 425°F. With parchment paper, line a large rimmed baking sheet.
2. In a small bowl, combine lemon juice, lemon zest, mustard, rosemary, honey, salt, and crushed red pepper. In another small bowl, combine panko, walnuts, and oil.
3. On the prepared baking sheet, place salmon. Over the fish, spread the mustard mixture and sprinkle with the panko mixture. Press to adhere. Coat lightly with cooking spray.
4. Bake until fish flakes set easily with a fork (8-12 minutes).
5. Sprinkle with parsley and serve with lemon wedges, if desired.

SNACKS
RECIPES

CHARCUTERIE BISTRO LUNCH BOX

Serving size: 1 box
Servings per recipe: 1
Calories: 452
Preparation time: 5 minutes
Cooking time: 0 minute

Carbs: 64.7 g Proteins: 16.9 g Fats: 17.1 g

INGREDIENTS

- Prosciutto slice - 1
- Halved mozzarella stick - 1
- Halved breadsticks- 2
- Dates - 2
- Grapes - ½ cup
- Large radishes - 2
- Halved or 4 slices English cucumber - (¼-inch)

DIRECTIONS

1. Cut prosciutto in half lengthwise. Wrap a slice around each portion of cheese, dates, breadsticks, grapes, and radishes (or cucumber) in a sealable container that has a 4-cup division. Refrigerate until ready to eat.

CLEMENTINE AND PISTACHIO RICOTTA

Serving size: ⅔ cup
Servings per recipe: 1
Calories: 178
Preparation time: 2 minutes
Cooking time: 5 minutes

Carbs: 14.6 g Proteins: 11.1 g Fats: 9 g

INGREDIENTS

- Part-skim ricotta - ⅓ cup
- Peeled and segmented clementine - 1
- Chopped pistachios - 2 tsp

DIRECTIONS

1. Into a small bowl, spoon ricotta and top it with clementine and pistachios.

CROCKPOT CHUNKY MONKEY PALEO TRAIL MIX RECIPE

Serving size: ¼ cup
Servings per recipe: 5-6 cups
Calories: 250
Preparation time: 5 minutes
Cooking time: 1 hour 30 minute

Carbs: 18 g Proteins: 4 g

INGREDIENTS

- Raw walnuts - 2 cups (halves or coarsely chopped)
- Raw cashew halves - 1 cup (whole almonds work, too)
- Unsweetened coconut flakes - 1 cup (be sure to get big FLAKES, not shredded)
- Coconut sugar - ⅓ cup
- Butter (cut in slices) - 1– 1.5 tbsp or at room temp 2 to 3 tbsp coconut oil to make vegan
- Vanilla or butter extract - 1 tbsp
- Unsweetened banana chips or freeze-dried banana slices - 6 oz.
- Dark chocolate chips or paleo fudge chunks - ½ cup to ⅔ cup (we used Enjoy life foods brand)

DIRECTIONS

1. In a crockpot, place nuts, coconut, sugar, vanilla, butter slices, and coconut oil. Mix all these items and keep on high for 45-60 minutes. Don't forget to stir a few times. Check-in between to make sure coconut flakes do not burn. Lower the flame after 45 minutes if flakes cook faster or start turning brown.

2. Turn the flame to low and keep cooking for 20-30 minutes.

3. Take it off and place the contents of the crockpot on parchment paper to dry out. Ensure that it is cooled for a minimum of 15 minutes prior to adding the chocolate and banana chips.

4. Now add in the chocolate chips and banana chips and mix.

5. Unsweetened Banana chips can optionally be added to cook with coconut/nuts, instead of adding afterward. However, it will need stirring frequently. It must be cooked for only 45 minutes.

6. Store in a zip-lock bag or airtight container.

GARLIC HUMMUS

Serving size: ¼ cup
Servings per recipe: 8
Calories: ¼ cup
Preparation time: 10 minutes
Cooking time: 0 minutes

Carbs: 9.7 g Proteins: 3.7 g Fats: 11.9 g

INGREDIENTS

- No-salt-added chickpeas - (15 ounces)
- Tahini - ¼ cup
- Extra-virgin olive oil - ¼ cup
- Lemon juice - ¼ cup
- Garlic clove - 1
- Ground cumin - 1 tsp
- Chili powder - ½ tsp
- Salt - ½ tsp

DIRECTIONS

1. Drain chickpeas, retaining ¼ cup of the liquid. Move the reserved liquid and chickpeas to a food processor.
2. Now add lemon juice, tahini, oil, garlic, cumin, chili powder, and salt.
3. Keep pureeing for 2-3 minutes or until very smooth.

HEALTHY AVOCADO CILANTRO WHITE BEAN DIP

Serving size: 2 cups dip with 2 heaping tbsp serving
Servings per recipe: 6
Calories: 144
Preparation time: 10 minutes
Cooking time: 5 minutes

Carbs: 18 g Proteins: 6 g Fats: 5 g

INGREDIENTS

- Organic cannellini beans - (approx. 15 oz)
- Large ripe avocado - 1
- Sour cream - 2 tbsp
- Jalapeno slices - 2 tbsp
- Garlic cloves - 2
- Fresh spinach - ½ cup (just grab a handful!)
- Fresh lime juice - 2-3 tbsp
- Fresh cilantro plus extra to taste - 2 tbsp
- Olive oil plus extra to garnish - 2 tbsp
- Ground cumin - ½ tsp
- Salt - ¼ tsp

DIRECTIONS

1. In a large food processor, place all dip ingredients. Keep processing until smooth.
2. It can be served at once or be covered and refrigerated until ready to use.
3. You can garnish with sliced cherry tomatoes, cilantro, and red onions.
4. Serve with veggies, Organics Blue Corn Tortilla chips with flaxseed, or Organics Pita Crackers.

HOMEMADE GRANOLA BARS (GLUTEN-FREE, VEGAN, DAIRY-FREE)

Serving size: 1
Servings per recipe: 12 bars
Calories: 209
Preparation time: 5 minutes
Cooking time: 1 hour 15 minutes

Carbs: 20.5 g Proteins: 8.0 g Fats: 11.6 g

INGREDIENTS

- Dried mulberries, chopped - ⅓ cup
- Dried strawberries, chopped - ⅓ cup
- Raw cashews, chopped - ½ cup
- Organic peanut butter - ½ cup
- Large ripe bananas, mashed- 2
- Raw sunflower seeds - ⅓ cup
- Organic hemp protein powder - 2 tbsp
- Gluten-free rolled oats - 1 cup
- Organic flaxseed meal - 2 tbsp

DIRECTIONS

1. Heat oven beforehand to 350°F. Use parchment paper and line an 8X8 square baking pan.
2. Combine the peanut butter and mashed banana in a medium mixing bowl using a manual mixer or an electric whisk.
3. Now add the rest of the ingredients to the bowl.
4. Using a spatula, mix the ingredients until they are well combined and a homogeneous mixture becomes obtainable.
5. Move the mixture to the baking pan. Press it down with a spatula until it is uniform and flat on all sides.
6. Bake it for around 25-30 minutes. Allow the granola to cool for a minimum of 40-45 minutes prior to removing it from the pan and cutting into bars.
7. Bars should be wrapped in wax paper and stored in the fridge in an airtight container for up to one week.

HUMMUS

Serving size: 1 small bowl
Servings per recipe: 8
Calories: 173 kcal
Preparation time: 12 minutes
Cooking time: 8 minutes

Carbs: 12 g Proteins: 4 g Fats: 13 g

INGREDIENTS

- Garlic cloves unpeeled - 2
- Chickpeas - 2 cups (342 g)
- Lemon juice - ¼ cup (60 ml)
- Tahini - ⅓ cup (67 g)
- Kosher salt - ½ tsp
- Extra-virgin olive oil plus more for drizzling - ¼ cup (60 ml)
- Paprika for garnish

DIRECTIONS

1. Take a small skillet and heat it over medium heat. Toast garlic to the point of it getting brown. Shake the pan in between. Peel garlic and set it aside.
2. Now drain the chickpeas; reserve ¼ cup of liquid.
3. Wash the chickpeas under cool water. Remove the outer skin using fingertips. If you want, you can keep the skin on, but it may affect the smoothness of your hummus.
4. Add ¼ cup of reserved chickpea liquid, tahini, and lemon juice to a blender or food processor.
5. Process it at high speed for a minute, until it becomes frothy.
6. Add garlic cloves, chickpeas, olive oil, and salt.
7. At high speed, process it for a minute. Scrape the sides down.
8. Next, process at high speed until it becomes smooth. This will take about 2 minutes.
9. Check the taste of the hummus. Flavor with more salt if you feel the need.
10. Serve without delay. Drizzle with olive oil and sprinkle with paprika.

HUMMUS, FETA, AND BELL PEPPER CRACKER

Serving size: I crispbread with topping
Servings per recipe: 1
Calories: 136
Preparation time: 10 minutes
Cooking time: 0 minutes

Carbs: 13.1 Proteins: 6 g Fats: 7.1 g

INGREDIENTS

- Hummus - 2 tbsp
- Large crispbread - 1 (whole-grain crispbread)
- Crumbled feta cheese - 2 tbsp
- Diced bell pepper - 2 tbsp

DIRECTIONS

1. On crispbread, spread hummus. Top with cheese and bell pepper.

LEMON HERB MEDITERRANEAN PASTA SALAD

Serving size: 1
Servings per recipe: 10 g
Calories: 108
Preparation time: 10 minutes
Cooking time: 15 minutes

Carbs: 3 g Proteins: 10 g Fats: 17.1 g

INGREDIENTS

- 12 oz. | 350 grams dry pasta (Penne)

FOR LEMON HERB DRESSING:

- Olive oil - ⅓ cup
- Fresh-squeezed lemon juice - 2 tbsp
- Red wine vinegar - 2 tbsp
- Water - 2 tbsp
- Finely chopped fresh parsley - 2 tbsp.
- Minced garlic - - 2 tsp
- Minced dried oregano - 2 tsp
- Dried basil - 1 tsp
- Salt ½ tsp
- Cracked pepper, to taste

INGREDIENTS

FOR SALAD:
- Romaine (or cos) lettuce leaves, washed and dried - 4 cups
- Large cucumber, diced - 1
- Avocado, peeled, pitted, and chopped - 1
- Large red pepper (or capsicum), deseeded and cut into thin strips - ½
- Grape or cherry tomatoes, halved - 9 oz. (250 grams)
- Thinly sliced red onion- ½
- Pitted Kalamata olives, sliced - ½ cup
- Sun-dried tomatoes packed in oil, drained - ⅓ cup
- Crumbled feta cheese - 5-6 tbsp

DIRECTIONS

1. In a large pot of salted water, boil pasta. Drain in a strainer or colander, then wash under cold water to take the heat out. Move the pasta to a large mixing bowl.
2. While pasta is boiling, prepare your dressing. In a large jug, whisk together all of the dressing/marinade ingredients.
3. In a salad bowl, add all the salad ingredients and pasta, and drizzle with a dressing. All the ingredients should be tossed together until everything is coated evenly in the dressing. Season with extra pepper and salt, if you feel like doing so. Serve at once.

MARINATED OLIVES AND FETA

Serving size: 2 tbsp
Servings per recipe: 12
Calories: 73
Preparation time: 10 minutes
Cooking time: 1 hour 10 minutes

Carbs: 2 g Proteins: 1.1 g Fats: 6.8 g

INGREDIENTS

- Sliced pitted olives, such as Kalamata or mixed Greek - 1 cup
- Diced feta cheese, preferably reduced-fat - ½ cup
- Extra-virgin olive oil - 2 tbsp
- Juice of 1 lemon - 1 zest
- Sliced cloves garlic - 2
- Chopped fresh rosemary - 1 tsp
- Crushed red pepper - 1 pinch
- Freshly ground pepper to taste

DIRECTIONS

1. In a medium bowl, combine feta, olives, oil, lemon juice, zest, garlic, rosemary, crushed red pepper, and black pepper.

MEDITERRANEAN PICNIC SNACKS

Serving size: 1¼ cup
Servings per recipe: 1
Calories: 197
Preparation time: 2 minutes
Cooking time: 3 minutes

Carbs: 22 g Proteins: 7.1 g Fats: 9.1 g

INGREDIENTS

- Crusty whole-wheat bread slice - 1 slice, cut into bite-size pieces
- Cherry tomatoes - 10
- Sliced aged cheese - ¼ ounce
- Oil-cured olives - 6

DIRECTIONS

1. In a portable container, combine bread pieces, cheese, olives, and tomatoes.

MINI GREEK PITA PIZZAS

Serving size: 1½ round
Servings per recipe: 12
Calories: 69 kcal
Preparation time: 10 minutes
Cooking time: 15 minutes

Carbs: 9 g Proteins: 2 g Fats: 3 g

INGREDIENTS

- Whole-wheat mini pitas or slide buns divided in half - 6
- Olive oil - 1 tbsp
- Homemade or store-bought hummus - ¼ cup
- Chopped tomato, seeded - ⅓ cup
- Chopped cucumber - ⅓ cup
- Chopped Kalamata olives - 3 tbsp
- Finely chopped red onion - 3 tbsp
- Crumbled feta cheese - 2 tbsp

DIRECTIONS

1. Preheat oven to 350°F.
2. Split 6 mini whole-wheat pitas or mini slider buns in half, to create 12 small rounds. Now place these rounds on a baking sheet.
3. Apply oil over each pita with a brush.
4. Now put in the oven and bake for 15 minutes or until they are crispy and lightly brown.
5. Take it out from the oven and apply a thin layer of hummus over each round, going right up to the edge.
6. On each top, place an equal amount of tomato, cucumber, red onion, olives, and feta. Serve without delay.

PEACH CAPRESE SKEWERS

Serving size: 3
Servings per recipe: 1
Calories: 143
Preparation time: 5
Cooking time: 0

Carbs: 17.3 g Proteins: 7.2 g Fats: 5.6 g

INGREDIENTS

- Medium peach, sliced - 1
- Cherry tomatoes - ½ cup
- Baby mozzarella balls - ¼ cup
- Fresh basil leaves - 4

DIRECTIONS

1. Thread peach slices onto skewers. Alternate mozzarella balls and basil onto skewers.

RICOTTA AND YOGURT PARFAIT

Serving size: 1¼ cup
Servings per recipe: 1
Calories: 272
Preparation time: 2 minutes
Cooking time: 5 minutes

Carbs: 25.1 g Proteins: 21.7 g Fats: 9.6 g

INGREDIENTS

- Non-fat vanilla Greek yogurt - ¾ cup
- Part-skim ricotta - ¼ cup
- Lemon zest - ½ tsp
- Raspberries - ¼ cup
- Slivered almonds - 1 tbsp
- Chia seeds - 1 tsp

DIRECTIONS

1. In a bowl, combine ricotta, yogurt, and lemon zest. Top with raspberries, almond, and chia seeds.

SAVORY FETA SPINACH AND SWEET RED PEPPER MUFFINS

Serving size: 2
Servings per recipe: 12
Calories: 240
Preparation time: 10 minutes
Cooking time: 25 minutes

Carbs: 13 g Proteins: 4 g Fats: 2 g

INGREDIENTS

- All-purpose flour (you can substitute partly with whole-wheat flour) - 2¾ cups
- Sugar - ¼ cup
- Baking powder - 2 tsp
- Paprika - 1 tsp
- Salt - ¾ tsp
- Low-fat milk - ¾ cup
- Extra-virgin olive oil - ½ cup
- Eggs - 2
- Fresh spinach, thinly sliced - 1¼ cups
- Crumbled feta - ¾ cup
- Florina peppers or other red pepper - ⅓ cup (drained and patted dry, jarred)

DIRECTIONS

1. Heat oven beforehand at 375°F.
2. Mix the dry ingredients: flour, sugar, baking powder, paprika, and salt.
3. Mix the olive oil, eggs, and milk in another bowl.
4. Now add the wet ingredients to the dry ingredients and keep mixing with a wooden spoon until blended. The dough will become thick.
5. Mix gently after adding feta, spinach, and peppers. Continue until all ingredients are spread thoroughly in the whole mixture.
6. Now divide the mixture in a muffin pan that you have lined with cupcake/muffin liners. Use a silicone muffin tray and grease it with a little olive oil. The oil should be enough for 12 medium muffins.
7. Next, bake it for about 25 minutes. Take it out when a toothpick comes out clear when inserted in the muffin.
8. Leave them to cool for 10 minutes and then remove them from the tray. Let them cool a couple of hours before you serve them.

SMOKED SALMON, AVOCADO, AND CUCUMBER BITES

Serving size: 3 bites
Servings per recipe: 12 bites
Calories: 46
Preparation time: 2 minutes
Cooking time: 8 minutes

Carbs: 2 g Proteins: 2 Fats: 3 g

INGREDIENTS

- Medium cucumber - 1
- Large avocado, peeled and pit removed - 1
- Lime juice - ½ tbsp
- Smoked salmon - 6 oz
- Chives, for garnish
- Black pepper, for garnish

DIRECTIONS

1. Using a serrated knife, slice the cucumber about ¼ inch thick and lay flat on a serving plate.
2. Next, put the avocado and lime juice in a bowl and use a fork to mash until creamy.
3. Now assemble the bites and spread a small quantity of avocado on each cucumber. Then top with a thin slice of smoked salmon.
4. Now dress each bite with finely chopped chives and cracked black pepper. Serve at once.

TOMATO-BASIL SKEWERS

Serving size: 1 skewer
Servings per recipe: 16
Calories: 46
Preparation time: 10 minutes
Cooking time: 0 minutes

Carbs: 1 g Proteins: 2.8 g Fats: 3.3 g

INGREDIENTS

- Small fresh mozzarella balls - 16
- Fresh basil leaves - 16
- Cherry tomatoes - 16
- Extra-virgin olive oil, to drizzle - 1 tsp
- Coarse salt and freshly ground pepper - 1/ to taste

DIRECTIONS

1. Place mozzarella, basil, and tomatoes on a small skewer.
2. Drizzle with oil and sprinkle with pepper and salt.

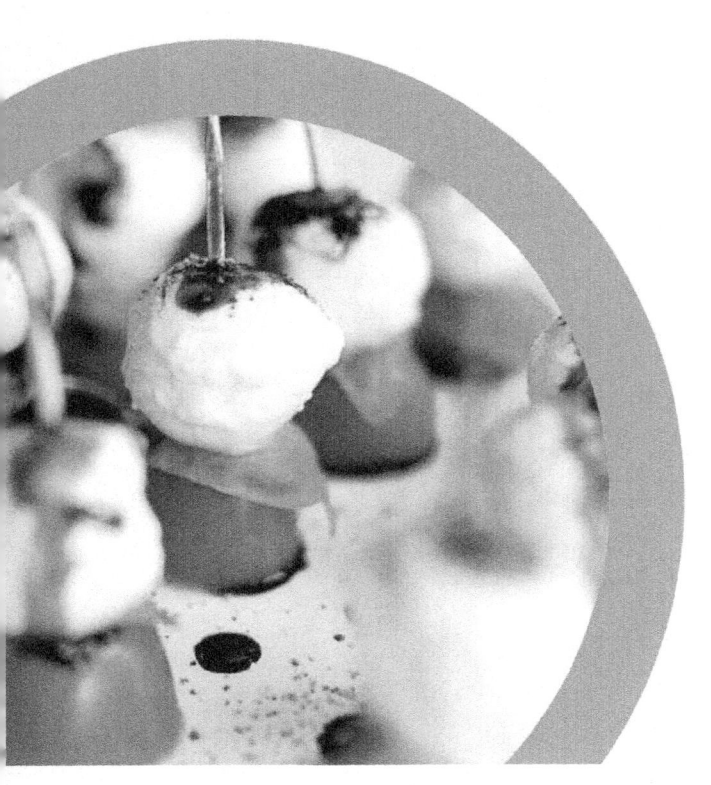

15-MINUTE MEDITERRANEAN CHICKPEA SALAD

Serving size: 1
Servings per recipe: 4
Calories: 196
Preparation time: 15 minutes
Cooking time: 5 minute

Carbs: 22g Proteins: 7 g Fats: 11 g

INGREDIENTS

- Chickpeas - 1.15 oz (drained, rinsed, and loose shells removed)
- Cherry tomatoes, halved - 1 pint
- Finely chopped cucumber - ½
- Sliced black olives - ¼ cup
- Herbed feta or plain - ¼ cup
- Juice of - 1 lemon
- Extra-virgin olive oil - 2 tbsp
- Red wine vinegar - 1 tbsp
- Fresh parsley, finely chopped - ¼ cup
- Fresh basil, finely chopped - 3 tbsp
- Garlic powder - ¼ tsp
- Pinch of sea salt and black pepper

DIRECTIONS

1. Everything is to be combined in a large bowl. Toss well to combine. Your dish is ready to be served.

An Appeal from the Publisher

Hello wonderful reader!

We hope you are enjoying this book.

We wanted to let you know that you have made an impact on many lives by reading this book.

Just to give you a brief introduction: We are a small publishing company with a team of 8 writers and 2 editors.

Most of our employees come from financially weaker section and our company is the only means they support their families. This is our way of giving back to the society.

We don't have the giant advertising budgets that many other publishers and businesses do online.

So, one way that you can really support our mission and our business is by leaving us a review on this book.

For a small company like us, getting reviews (especially on Amazon) means we can submit our books for advertising.

This means we can actually sell a few copies from time to time and make a bigger impact on the society as a whole. So, every review means a lot to us.

We can't THANK YOU enough for this!

Made in the USA
Monee, IL
10 March 2021